Praise for *Fatima's Touch*

Tamam Kahn has done a fine job of portraying Fatima, her family and the historical milieu. This is the best of her work that I have seen so far. These are important pages for those who are ignorant of the whole cultural history, and also because the historical record is so spotty, so ravaged, so dismissive. This deserves to be known, and I congratulate her on the research and artistry of the poems and the courage and determination of this admirable achievement.

–Fred Chappell, Former Poet Laureate of North Carolina,
author *of Shadow Box* and *I Am One of You Forever.*

Tamam Kahn has undertaken, in a sequence of poems interspersed with prose texts, to give English-speaking readers a sense of the transcendent, plural meanings of the life and legends of Fatima, daughter of the Prophet Mohammed. Comparable in scope to Assia Djebbar's *Loin de Médine* in its introducing Westerners to the origins of Islam, and the vital importance of women in its foundation, it is also a magisterial accomplishment as poetry, marrying narrative power to formal virtuosity, memorable and conducive to meditation.

–Marilyn Hacker, National Book Award Winner,
author of *A Stranger's Mirror.*

In Fatima's Touch, Tamam Kahn liberates the woman and prophet Fatima from layers of hagiography, idealization that have made her into an Islamic icon. Tamam's poetry reveals her own deep inner process as well as her intuitive grasp of what it means to be an inspired woman, challenged by the restrictions of both religion and patriarchal culture. Even if you don't normally read poetry, you will find this a moving and eloquent journey.

–Neil Douglas-Klotz, author of *The Sufi Book of Life* and *Desert Wisdom*

We need to learn devotion to the holy ones, and especially the women. Tamam Kahn helps us to connect with the beloved Fatima. May we ask our minds and hearts to look toward such examples of Blessed Humanity.

–Kabir Helminski, author of *Living Presence,*
The Knowing Heart, and many translations of Rumi.

Fatima's Touch

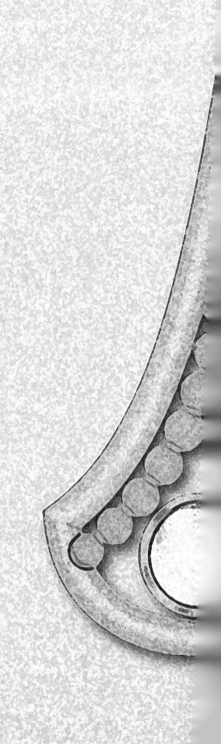

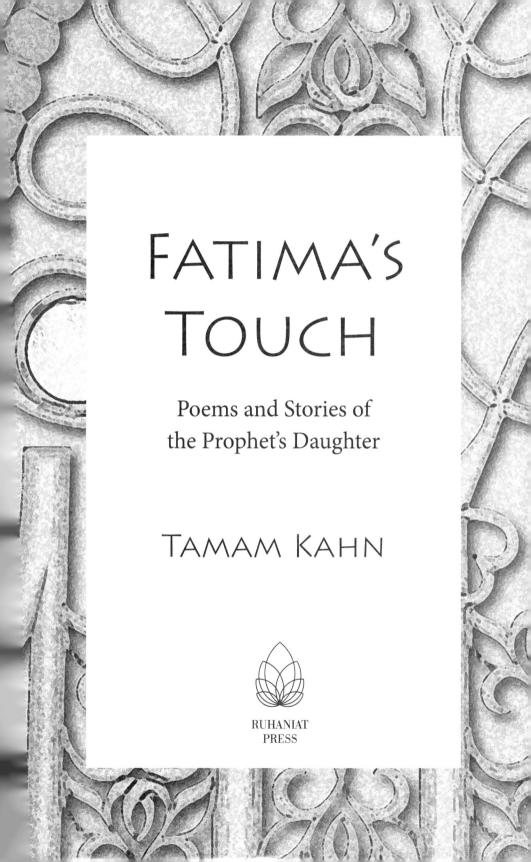

FATIMA'S TOUCH

Poems and Stories of
the Prophet's Daughter

TAMAM KAHN

RUHANIAT
PRESS

Book and cover design by Hauke Jelaluddin Sturm
www.designconsort.de.
Author photograph by Shabda Kahn
Printed in the United States of America

ISBN 978-0-9973999-0-5
Library of Congress Control Number 2016945724
Library of Congress Cataloging in Publication Data
1. Poetry 2. Biography
Title: Fatima's Touch: Poems and Stories of the Prophet's Daughter/ Tamam Kahn
Includes bibliographical references

Ruhaniat Press
Sufi Ruhaniat International
410 Precita Avenue
San Francisco, CA 94110
https://completeword.wordpress.com/fatimas-touch/

Contents

‡ metrical poems (33)

Acknowledgements

This book is dedicated to my son Solomon Samuel Kahn
7/11/77–1/31/12

Great thanks to my husband, Shabda. Without his love and support there would be no book. I offer warm appreciation to Dr. Arthur Buehler who invited me to join him on this path, telling the life of Fatima, and offered me his Arabic translations and important reflections on every poem. Poet and mentor, Annie Finch, believed in the importance of telling the story of this great woman, and supplied brilliant metrical editing in this writing.

Gratitude to Wendy Taylor Carlisle my poetry muse and excellent editor, Fred Chappell for wise corrections, Jelehla Ziemba, who coaxed the sentence to slide smoothly along. Appreciation to Marilyn Hacker, Dr. David D. Peck, Neil Saadi Douglas-Klotz, Lesley Hazelton, Coleman Barks, Basira Beardsworth, Baiba Strads, Kyra Epstein, Imam Bilal Hyde, Ayat Kindschi, Justen Ahren of *Noepe Center for Literary Arts*, Abraham Sussman, Allan and Alexandra Cole, Lorna Knowles Blake, Daisy Khan, Kabir Helminski, and Barbara Wirth with the Asian Art Museum of San Francisco. Respectful recognition goes to Cemalnur Sargut from Istanbul.

Special thanks to Lama Palden Alioto for her generosity, Ragdale Residency (in the care of Regin Igloria and Susan Tillett) and Jentel Artist Residency (Neltje, Mary Jane Edwards and Lynn Reeves) —all for offering me supportive locations to write and revise the poems in this book.

I offer appreciation to all my Sufi friends and family who held faith in this project reaching completion, especially Hauke Jelaluddin Sturm, who arranged the words into a beautiful book.

Preface

She is from my flesh, the light of my eye and the fruit of my heart.
Prophet Muhammad[1]

Millions of Muslims the world over wear silver and gold pendants in the shape of Fatima's hand as blessing and protection. Her hand is reproduced in jewelry, ceramics, paintings, tapestries and T-shirts, and is even used in a cellphone advertisement in Morocco. It is the hand-of-protection throughout the Muslim world.

Yet most Americans know her name only because of a Christian shrine in a small town in Portugal named for Muhammad's favorite daughter.[2] Near this shrine, linked to the Virgin Mary known as Our Lady of Fatima, the Blessed Virgin appeared to three girls in 1917. Fatima al-Zahra. Who was she? And why do we in the West seem to know so little about the woman whom many Muslims revere and treasure as deeply as Christians do Mary?

What should Americans know about Fatima? Begin with her father, Muhammad the Prophet of Islam. He lived in Mecca, Arabia in the first two decades of the seventh century and worked as a commercial caravan leader for a businesswoman named Khadija. They married. Historians agree that Fatima was born to Khadija and Muhammad, the man who received Revelation from God. Khadija, like her husband, came from a well-respected family. When Fatima's father, Prophet Muhammad, began to receive Revelation and speak of One God, Khadija supported him in every possible way, while the traditional business establishment turned most of the city against him. His words impacted both their traditions and finances.

In 622 CE, two years after Khadija's death, Muhammad fled 300 miles north to Medina and then sent for Fatima. Still a girl dependent on her father, she was uprooted and taken from the life she knew. Muhammad's family and followers established a new community and Fatima was married to her cousin, Ali. They raised their four children in Medina as the message of Prophet Muhammad grew and spread. Fatima lived for only a short time after her father's death in 632.[3] Within decades those close to Muhammad became deeply divided.

But what of the biographical particulars of Fatima's life? There are numerous sources that open surprisingly colorful moments. We know of the early days of Islam through quotations and anecdotes repeated by those who lived close to Muhammad. These stories and sayings, called *hadith,* are transmissions of what Muhammad and his family and companions, were supposed to have done and said, and how the Islamic world understands their history. In the years following the Prophet's death these hadith were treasured, handed down carefully by people who memorized the details and occasionally wrote them down. The written record was filtered through what was thought to be significant or edifying.[4]

My work here as a poet is to honor what has been told, which often reads as conflicting information. I write to make Fatima accessible. I visit both the Sunni and Shia hadith (differences will be discussed in the introduction) and appreciate their messages, but, most importantly, I write to join this contentious family through the quiet power of poems. Poetry has a way of nudging sense and meaning inside a stream of words, the way water runs under the desert sand— to green an oasis.

Thirty-three of the poems are written in meter, like the repetition and variations of drumbeats, recalling a time when the written word was marginal and poetry was spoken in easy-to-remember patterns. Books of poems rarely refer to these patterns overtly, but here they become part of the connection to the rhythms of the time, flowing (at best) unnoticed.

I have followed the Sufi path for forty years. To me, Sufism is the fragrance over the flowers of religion. My husband, Shabda, and I have traveled widely among the mystics in North Africa, the Middle East and India. For the last fifteen years I have been exploring the stories of the first women in what would become *Islam*—(from *salaam*). The word *Islam* is associated with "… the inner state that causes the feeling of peaceful surrender to the protection, safety, and healing of the Divine."[5] In the fall of 2012, Shabda and I planned a trip to Turkey. I asked everyone I could think of—Sufis, publishers, scholars, professors— for names of those in Istanbul knowledgeable about Fatima al-Zahra. Without exception, they all directed me to Cemâlnur Sargut, female Sufi teacher and scholar who "aims … to see all [humanity] as one without discriminating between genders, religions, sects or outlooks."[6]

We met on a warm autumn day at her house, a ferry ride from our hotel. We spoke for more than an hour. I said I was writing a book of poems about Fatima. I had questions for her, which she answered. Toward the end of the conversation, I shared with her that my thirty-four year old son, Solomon, had died in a car accident in Bangkok that year, two years into my writing these poems.

After I told my story, she said: "It is because of the pain that you are given with the loss of your son that you have permission to do this work. You should be grateful that Hazrat Fatima has allowed you to speak for her." I left that meeting feeling strong guidance, and the urge to rewrite some of my poetry. Plato once said: "Poetry is nearer to vital truth than history is." That day, I moved to a layer deeper than scholarship. I am in Fatima's hands. May this collection of poems offer glimpses of her life and how she is remembered. May it bring the reader nearer to Fatima.

Introduction

People are trapped in history and history is trapped in them.
James A. Baldwin

Fatima lived before there were Shia and Sunni divisions in the Muslim community. The rift between those known as Shia and those called Sunni occurred in the first few centuries after Prophet Muhammad's death (632 CE). The Shia were followers of Ali, Fatima's husband who became Imam Ali, the fourth caliph. The Sunni were those who championed the first three caliphs: Abu Bakr, Umar, and Uthman. This sectarian perspective justifies modern political agendas and continues to tear Islam apart.

One event that proved formative in the Shia/Sunni divide involved Fatima's son, Husayn. In the year 680 CE, on the day known as *Asura*, in the area called Karbala in what today is Iraq, a large military force representing the reigning caliph, Yazid, surrounded Fatima's last living son and the men, women and children traveling with him. After starving the travelers and refusing them water, Yazid's troops attacked Husayn. In the slaughter that followed, Husayn was beheaded and his followers decimated.[1] Women and child prisoners were marched for days across the desert to Damascus. To understand the significance to the Shia of the martyrdom at Karbala is to let these words penetrate deeply: *Every day is Asura and every land is Karbala.* No one puts this agony to rest; no one gets over it.

While many Shia believe Husayn sacrificed himself for all Muslims, the Sunni were also shocked by Karbala, but they don't focus on it, and they make up about 80 percent of the Muslim world. The Sunni haven't taken Karbala, Husayn—and by extension, Fatima—into their religious core. They concentrate, instead, on the example given by Prophet Muhammad, and honor his daughter. Consequently, their view of Fatima is different in key respects.

It follows from these divergent viewpoints that Fatima's life story often contains conflicting material. After Karbala, a much stronger view of Fatima, who died decades before—emerges. The following image shines from the Shia hadith (the writings of the *ahl al-Bayt*, the Prophet's close family): *The roof of Fatima's house is God's Holy Throne.*[2] Central to the Shia admiration is the retelling of Fatima's impassioned sermon at the mosque following her father's death. From today's perspective, for a woman to speak to both women and men in a mosque is a shocking accomplishment never mentioned in Sunni chronicles. The Sunni stories speak instead of her closeness to her father, wifely duties, poverty, hard work and blistered hands.

Hers is not a straightforward story. It is a quarrel among Muslims soaked in lethal bitterness.

Part One

A Cup of Grace

Sacred Names

Fatima is five or six years old, youngest of four daughters, living comfortably in a house where her mother manages a profitable international caravan business. Her home in the middle of Mecca is a hub of activity with servants as well as visiting relatives and successful townspeople. Muhammad, her father, is often at home, and the house has a yard where the large animals, horses and camels, are stabled. In this poem she wanders outside to sit in dust and palm duff, polishing her father's shoes to demonstrate her devoted service. He, in turn, appreciates her. That horizontal respect is close to the Sunni view of Muhammad, his daughters and Khadija, his only wife for 25 years. He honors them.

On the other hand, the Shia elevate Fatima and invest her with sacred qualities made manifest in her many names—a vertical ladder of light. "Sacred Names" brings the two impressions of this young Meccan girl together.

Habibi – sweetie, loved one (Arabic).

SACRED NAMES

For Oona

Five-year-old Fatima playing alone—
hiding in curtains, counting to ten,
yelling in Arabic: "here I come!"
LIGHT OF HEAVEN, here I come!"
PURE. BRAVE. GLORIFIED. SHINING.
"They'll call me these names when I get to heaven."
KNOWLEDGEABLE. SHE-WHO-SATIFIES-GOD.

Fatima at the door recites: THE-PATIENT-ONE. CHASTE.
She takes up one of her father's sandals
to slip on her small foot, then stands
in the other shoe, clunks into the back yard.
CLEAN. She scuffs up a dust cloud. IMMACULATE.
She squats in palm duff, RADIANT. pulls at each sandal-strap
and examines each dusty shoe, concentrates. GENTLE.

VIRTUOUS. PROTECTED. VIRGINAL. She spits and polishes
the leather with the front of her tunic. FRIEND-OF-GOD.
She smiles at the camel eating next to her. AFFECTIONATE.
"You are my *habibi*," she coos to him. Her clothes are
dirty, soiled from His shoes. STAINLESS.
Her sticky fingers smear her face. BEAUTIFUL.

Muhammad stands in the doorway, arms folded,
delight all over his face. "O, Zahra, DAUGHTER-OF-LIGHT.
I am BLESSED with how GENEROUS you are. My shoes.
How you care for them! Fatima gives him a long look:
WISE. VICTORIOUS. SATISFIED. MOTHER-OF-HER-FATHER.

Father, may I walk with you wherever you walk.

3

One Morning in Sayfad-din's Kitchen

In 2014, I spent a week in Amman Jordan with scholar Arthur Buehler. He translated and shared Shia and Sunni references including *The Encyclopedia of Fatima al-Zahra* in twenty-five volumes in Arabic, from Qumm, Iran. Among the treasures of that encyclopedia were little known *hadith:* oral anecdotes recalling the words and deeds of Muhammad, transcribed centuries ago.

In my working notebook are two photographs of fifteenth-century Turkish miniatures. They show Fatima with blank white paint substituted for her face. The command not to show Fatima with a human face has been explained in this way: our eyes are not refined enough to glimpse her features. The moon-like white oval instead suggests Fatima's illumination and divine Grace. Neither Sunni nor Shia depict the face of Fatima.

I ask myself: does this artistic convention convey respect, or do the missing features separate us from her humanness?

4

ONE MORNING IN SAYFAD-DIN'S KITCHEN

Looking down into milk before I pour it,
there is Fatima's face—a whitened roundness.
Milk we bought in Amman, a nearby market;
standard Arabic words surround the bottle,
translate: "Fresh milk from cows, completely pure, whole."

Pour. My reasonable-self's requesting. *Pour now,
past the bottle's blue sealing ring.* Her face, all
free of womanly features—human features—
chilled and stark. Now I tip it gently. Brimming,
white, contained by the cup, all safe, encircled.

Drink! My God, I am lifting milk and smiling.

*This is what you are meant to do—yes. Drink and
stay alert to the drinking. Sip. Be nourished.
Write of Fatima's life, her world. Her presence.*

Fruit-of-the-Heart

n the tale of the Prophet riding *Buraq,* a winged steed with a human face, to the heavens, the Sufis see a metaphor for traveling on the breath into a deep state. Most versions of the story have him meeting with God and the prophets and receiving instructions for prayer. A handful of Shia and Sunni scholars connect this narration with Fatima's conception.[1]

In this version, Angel Gabriel offered him fruit. He ate and carried the heavenly seed of Fatima, which blossomed when he returned home.

ثمر الفؤاد

In tracing the Arabic for *fruit,* definitions lead from *al-thamar* (fruit) *to thamar-al-fuad,* (fruit-of–the-heart.)[2] I was amazed to see that this phrase was also used to refer to children or grandchildren, which brings the legend full circle.

FRUIT-OF-THE-HEART: A SONNET

Muhammad rode *Buraq* to paradise.
Right there the angel handed him sweet fruit,
al-thamar, ripe as moonrise. He was wise,
ate deeply, taking in God's gift, renewed
by love seeds ripe and rushing to be sown
on earth. That message rose in him. He went.
Turned home to wife Khadija, anchor on
his night-flight. He held her with intent
and urgency to share this *golden glow*,
the swinging, singing; being fed by God
disguised, all synchronized from head to toe
in praise and praise unflawed, sky seed-to-pod
—fruition. Stars rose and lit horizon's rim, a
blessed and best conception night for Fatima.

Dates

Fatima's timeline is a matter of controversy that tangles her history.[1] Sunni and Shia biographers quarrel over a ten-year discrepancy, with the Sunni insisting on earlier markers. Her life would be very different if she spent her early childhood in the calm before Muhammad became an enemy of the businessmen running Mecca. More than one "authentic" version of her life's important events makes it extremely difficult to write about Fatima in prose. Poetry can play in the differences.

In the first three couplets, the first line offers the Sunni view, the second line the Shia perspective.

Dates and butter were a favorite food for Muhammad.
Anbara Medina – a type of date known for its sweet taste and healing properties.

Dates

Fatima's born when her mother is forty.
Fatima's born when her mother is fifty years old.

Fatima's is five when Revelation gathers up her family.
Fatima's born after Revelation, sweet as dates and butter.

Fatima bears Hasan at twenty.
Fatima bears Hasan at ten.

It's agreed. Fatima *appears in God's throne room* in 632.
In the palmary, sharp beaked birds fight over fresh dates.

Fatima eats no more *Anbara Medinas*.
Her husband and children taste terrible loss.

Palm fronds shade her name under a gleam of fruit.

The Silver Hand

The *Hand of Fatima* can be worn as an amulet and used as a sign of protection. It is said in Morocco: a house protected by The *Hand of Fatima* will not catch fire. The same shaped hand is worn by Jews—called a *hamsah,* used for protection against the evil eye, and can be traced to ancient Mesopotamia. The Jews do not associate it with the Prophet's daughter, but this one symbol is venerated by both faiths.

I have read that the five fingers of this hand of honor represent Muhammad, Fatima, Ali, Hasan and Husayn. The same five people make up the a*hl al-bayt,* the "holy household" who are represented under "the cloak," in many stories.[1]
The traditional reading does not make allowance for Fatima's daughters, Zaynab and Umm Kulthum. I think Fatima would have wanted her daughters included.

al-falak – celestial sphere, star (orbit of), implies swimming as well as orbiting.

SILVER HAND

We forget the face
but wear the silver hand,
forget the look
of a lighthouse,
but recall the beam;
witness being lifted
on clear digits of light.

We concede
her rescuing face.
Like her father's,
we say, but we cannot
see either one.

Ya falak!
We swim as stars
in orbit round his
daughter, a lamp
of whispered mercy.

When she extends
her hand, we are
met in unforgettable
touch.

Delivery

On a cold November day during Ramadan 2003, we sat in my hotel room in Damascus—Nuha al-Abed, scholar, Mevlevi Sufi and I. She shared stories from generations of Syrian women in her family. She told me their legend of Fatima's birth.

Khadija began her labor alone. Then four ancient matriarchs, women-of-the-book all, honored her with their presence and help. Fatima was delivered by the sister of Moses, wife of Abraham, Mother of Jesus, and wife of the Pharaoh.[1] This is verified in a Shia source, while a Sunni scholar substitutes for Sara, wife of Abraham—Hawa, the wife of Adam, called by many in Islam, "Grandmother Eve."[2]

And how old was Khadija at Fatima's birth? Sources disagree. Since her marriage to Muhammad, she had already given birth to a son who died at birth and three other girls. She had to be younger than history claims.[3] To say a woman is "old" implies respect, which increases with age. Khadija was deeply respected.

Hijaz – western Arabia where Mecca and Medina are located.

DELIVERY

Who do you think delivered this baby?
Nuha, my friend from Syria, asked me.
They were there—The Women of the Book!
the sister of Moses, the Pharaoh's spouse,
Abraham's wife and the Mother of Jesus—
Kulthum, Asiya, Sara, Maryam —
they brought her forth.

Lets celebrate the birth of Fatima with a cake,
whipped and spooned and baked perfectly.
Frosted and layered with date cream and butter.
It's heavenly. Confections shimmer like *Hijaz* stars.
There is something grim about childbirth
In the seventh century. After such labor
a woman like Khadija with a bed full of children
has earned the perfect cake, a birth cake,
with a layer for each pair of soothing hands.

Ghazal

A man of the Quraysh …*brought a sheep's entrails, which he then threw over my head while I was prostrate in prayer. Fatima came and washed it off.*[1] These words were spoken by Prophet Muhammad, and passed down as *hadith*. The incident refers to the time the city fathers stirred up the public with their dislike of Muhammad's words and activities in Mecca. As long as Uncle Abu Talib lived (Muhammad's tribal protector), no one was allowed to harm him, but they could torment and ridicule him.

In line with Sunni biographical material on Fatima, this telling demonstrates practicality, seriousness and above all, the caretaking nature of Fatima—even as a child. "Muhammad's approach was one of gentleness, discernment, calm deliberation known as *hilm*… as well as an antidote to this kind of behavior."[2] He would have taught her to respond in the spirit of *hilm*.

GHAZAL

Some Meccans boast about their dirty work over and over,
fling entrails at her father's back in mirth, over and over.

With child's small hands she cleans him as he bends
to pray. Laughter follows each man's curse, over and over.

Scribes say she calls the wrath of God on all these brutes.
Yet she is schooled in kindness from the first, over and over.

Humiliation and disgust, and yet this girl can hold
her tongue. She's washed in love, immersed in it over and over.

She lives instructed by the strife; Muhammad's trials—
scapegoated, badgered, even hurt, over and over.

They call Fatima the *Mother of Her Father.* Her task blessed
by what she does, attentive and alert—over and over.

Planned Famine: Mecca around the year 617

After many attempts to suppress or drive away Muhammad and his followers, the Meccan chiefs isolated the Muslim community and created an embargo to starve them out of Mecca. It lasted two years. Now and then, underground supporters would risk sending a laden mule to their communal dwellings. There was no regular source of food. Fatima endured this situation, which contributed to her mother Khadija's illness and death soon after restrictions were lifted.

PLANNED FAMINE: MECCA, AROUND THE YEAR 617

No one in Mecca was allowed to... sell goods, including food and water, to any member of (Muhammad's clan).

Reza Aslan

There was a perpetual shortage of foods ...(that) bordered on famine.

Martin Lings

Hard to speak, in this raw-edged hunger, famine.
Blur it, blot it all out—reflection, logic.

> Nothing Fatima said would make a difference.
> Stealing food in her dreams, by day she begged at
> wells disguised as a nomad. Bowl and legs were
> shaking—anger and prayer, her tongue all bitten.
> She began to use Names-of-God for flavor,
> filled the family plates with light and scraps that
> seemed to brighten the children, soothe the mothers.

Yet the unyielding grave, they said, would call them:
Mother, Come to me! No one brought them, sent them
food unless it was smuggled. Chewed on leather.
Daylight rubbed all their dried-out eyes for water.
Twilight pushed down the shovel, served the graveyard.

Going On

Fatima's mother is respected by all Muslims. She is the matrix of love, wisdom, and generosity in this family. Now she is dying. Fatima and Muhammad attend her last hours. (According to the Sunnis she was fifteen when her mother died; the Shia say she's five years old.) Fatima asked, "Where is my mother?" Angel Gabriel: *Tell her Khadija is in a house of gold brocade, decorated in pearl. The columns are rubies. Mary, mother of Jesus is there too...*[1] The text adds that Khadija is positioned in paradise between two of the legendary women who helped deliver Fatima: Asiya, wife of Pharaoh, and Maryam, mother of Jesus.

What of Fatima? Perhaps as a fifteen-year-old, she might hang on fiercely to her mother's last moments on earth, even beg the day not to end. Khadija, like many women of that time, ran a business as well as her own household. She had been well-respected in Mecca. Fatima's extraordinary mother would no longer love and teach her or the next generation. I've given her age from the Sunni perspective. A five-year-old girl would just be asking: "Where is my mother?" She could not help Muhammad or wash her mother's body with the women friends, and prepare it for burial.

GOING ON

Fatima: Sun—don't set. Don't take the light. Now I'm asking. Let your ray touch down on her cheek, her breath inhaling father's words, and the message. Stop her very last exhale!

Father: Listen daughter, Gabriel has a message
               sent from God: Salaam to you. Know, your mother's
               joining Allah's praise-worthy splendor. This is
               verification.

Fatima: Heaven's angels, ancestors, death—pass by! She
               spoke my name not long ago, gently whispered
               it, engaging me. Now the sunlight journeys,
               leaves me in darkness.

Father: [He whispers now]: Paradise—concealed delights,
               lit by love. Khadija's house gleams, shaped with
               jewels and pearls, eternally. She's with Mary,
               Mother of Jesus.

Fatima: Mama's dead? I'm holding the day my captive,
               praying, touching and washing her with
               daylight's waters, hours and fragrant kisses—
               I tend her body.

Father: Let her go, and Fatima—help me wrap her,
               bury her, and celebrate all she gave you.
               Listen to the truth and accept this death—her
               threshold to heaven.

Fatima: Separation rips like a blade. I stitch both
               sides together. Pulled apart. Listen, Mama:
               twilight deepens. Here's my grief: you'll never
               watch, hold my children.

Shine

Fatima al-Zahra glowed. Her other name, *Zahra*, means "Radiant One."

> *Three times a day she shone with light... her face*
> *was shining in the morning prayer and on the people*
> *in their beds: the whiteness of that light entered*
> *their rooms in Medina and illuminated their walls...*
> *(At noon) the light of her face shone with a yellow*
> *color, and the glow lit the rooms.... At the end of the*
> *day, when the sun had set... Fatima's face radiated*
> *with redness (that) ...joyfully entered the rooms of*
> *the people.*[1]

This stunning visual description, with colored lights is among
the best of Shia metaphorical language demonstrating great
admiration for the woman who was Fatima. This calling of
the states of Fatima's consciousness, reminded me of Robert
Frost's poem, "Silken Tent," which begins: *She is as in a field*
a silken tent... I ended each line but one (of the 14 lines of the
sonnet) with the last word of the line used in his poem—*pole,*
ward, soul, cord... The polished vehicle of Frost's poetry carried
me into the mastery of Fatima's awareness. The attunement to
both Fatima and Frost prompted me to make the sonnet into a
single sentence, as is "Silken Tent."

SHINE

The shining happened every day, in tent
and hut, in all the rooms, and while the breeze
would linger, Zahra's glow, all white, relent-
lessly lit up each scene with light that squeezed
out dark—she sparked delight, a living pole
star—a lighthouse beaming, pointing toward
each heart as if to soothe and bleach the soul
of doubt as noon-prayer yellow sang a cord,

a citrine gem; that sound showed women bound
in Zahra's golden ties of love and thought,
while unity of sound went round and round
and reddened as the sun passed through the taut

line of the earth—red stayed in land and air;
while Zahra's face shone conscious and aware.

Jinn

The jinn – the "Hidden Ones" are part of folk culture, and were mentioned in Qur'an.[1]

Fatima's life story emphasizes her austerity, her lack of material possessions. This is somewhat contradicted by commentary from the *Encyclopedia of Fatima,* (vol. 17) "Rings and Seals." This section claims she had several rings made of silver. One was engraved: *Praise God for restraining the jinn from speaking.*[2]

When Muhammad was on Mount Hira, Gabriel squeezed him and forced him to recite the first words of Revelation. Muhammad became afraid that he was possessed by the jinn or what is known as the *genii* in the West.[3]

JINN

Praise God for restraining the jinn from speaking.

Past generations claim dubious allies
genii or jinn pressing dark inspiration.

That's what Muhammad was worried about once
when Gabriel made him recite Revelation.

What if one jinn, all unnoticed, should wriggle
in between Fatima's hands while she supplicates?

Thanks to the words on the ring, he'd be speechless,
blinded and stunned as the angels threw stars at him.

Part Two

In Exile

Wild Honey of Adab

*A*dab is the basic principle of social interaction in the Middle East. It includes refined behavior, politeness, consideration for others, and doing the right thing at the right time for the right reason. Extended to strangers as well as community, good adab is a point of honor for an individual.

This is an important reference, since Aisha is speaking, describing a sweet pattern of connection between her husband, Muhammad, and his daughter, Fatima. In the Sunni hadith Aisha and Fatima are often shown as compatible.[1] This picture of Muhammad's adab, greeting and offering his daughter his own seat is an indication of their love and respect for each other.

Waggle dance is a term used in beekeeping and ethnology for a particular figure-eight movement of the honey bee, communicating the direction of food.

WILD HONEY OF ADAB

Was there ever a better gesture for us than this? The way
Muhammad rises when Fatima enters the room
and takes her hand to kiss it, then indicates his seat to her.

At her house, she reciprocates. Each garland of respect
reveals the wild honey of adab;
inflorescent meadows spreading out, scented

with grace. Since we know the sting of a shrug,
how kindness can pivot and leave the room without a glance—
become the Bee Keeper. Stretch toward the buzz of others,

watch over each hive as the honey bees waggle.
Move slow, bee veil lowered. Honor the queen,
and hand a sweet jar to everyone you meet.

Escape into Exile

There are several versions of Fatima's journey from Mecca to Medina—a three-hundred-mile ride. Most accounts don't have Ali bringing the three women to Medina. This one is led by Ali and includes his mother, cousin and Fatima al-Zahra.[1] The Shia here tell that Muhammad sent a message to Ali from Medina to come quickly, leave at night and bring the three Fatimas.

A traditional account by Ibn Kathir lists Fatima, her sister Umm Kulthum, Umm Ayman, Aisha and her brother, Abd' Allah traveling with guides, Zayd and Abu Rafi.[2]

A *howdah* is a sheltered platform often mounted on a camel. *Red-legged-clump-wing* is the name that pre-Islamic poets gave to the ostrich. This bird lived in Arabia until the twentieth century, and was regarded by early desert Bedouin as a relative of the camel.
Rain-stars refer to the time of the rainy season.
Barwaq is a small white wild flower found in sand or gravelly depressions in Arabia.
Ride the wing of the ostrich means "to devote one self whole-heartedly to something."

Escape into Exile

for Wendy TC

I lift this exile poem into a *howdah,*
then tuck the shawl around Ali's mother.
I write of rarest rain for setting out,
      then turn aside eight chasers with a ploy.

Under the wind-wail I nudge each horse and camel
      on to a road as mud dries into dust.
I place red rocks and wells along the path
      where dull brown weeds sing into parching thirst.

I shout—*O ostrich! Red-legged-clump-wing*—
salute the bird, her nest of shiny eggs.
      How good they taste. Here is a meal at last.

I bloom, as strong as desert-white *barwaq.*
 Fatima *rides the wing* with Ali. Bare hills
      around, gowned in mirage appear, then fade.

I turn, display the green of orchard palms
Medina—all the bushes nod, a boy
calls out: *They're here!* This moment holds
      both past and future. I've come far enough.

29

Remedy For Fire

Prophet Muhammad said: "I called my daughter Fatima because God, powerful and lofty, has separated her and separated those who love her from the fire."[1] Shia and Sunni sources speak of her pure life. Because of that, God has forbidden that Fatima or her offspring experience the fires of hell. On the day of judgment "…those who love Fatima will cling to the hem of her cloak and be delivered from the fire…"[2]

When I was working on this poem I was near the Rocky Mountains in northern Wyoming in a spring snowfall. It felt chaste and serene, very far from fire in all its aspects.

REMEDY FOR FIRE

You who love her avoid the burn; destructive

arson—something called sin. She's spraying rain you
splash in. Fatima welcomes crusty white and
virgin blue snow-banks; calls to whirling flurries,
fresh and chaste as a zero. Fire is finished.

Inscribed in Light

Imagine timeless graffiti that predates even Adam and Eve,
and tells of Fatima reaching excellence as well as perfection.
Some Sunni scholars give this honor to the daughter of the
Prophet. In the oldest Shia record Muhammad as he is dying,
tells his daughter: *You are the leader of the women of paradise.*[1]
Sayyid, as a term of high respect, can mean lord or master, or
refer to descendants of the Prophet but there is not a parallel
translation for the feminine, *sayyida* (here translated *leader.*)

Now imagine words stating Fatima's lofty position written in
light on the leg of God's throne. It's said that Adam read it and
mentioned it to Muhammad when he was on his Night Journey
through the seven heavens.[2] Here "paradise" expands into
worlds, not just ours but further, much further, beyond what
we know and experience, beyond the stars. The story grows.
Afran-the-Jinn said Iblis, the fallen angel, saw Fatima's name on
God's throne seven thousand years before God created Adam.
He pleaded with God to take him from hell's fire in the name of
Fatima and her family.[3]

It is from here on the supporting throne of God—which the
Sufis would say is the "One Heart"— that Fatima reaches out
to women of the worlds: her life's example is her message.

INSCRIBED IN LIGHT

Here on one leg of God's vast throne
these ancient words inscribed in light

Fatima, sayyida for women of the worlds

sayyida, unnamable woman's blessing

sayyida a prodigious mandate

yet Allah extends his glory to Fatima

her name and task precisely written
touched by the breeze from a thousand wings.

Gift of Prayer

S unni stories of Fatima emphasize her poverty and hardship.
Not long after she and Ali were married, prosperity seemed
distant from their community in Medina. Fatima went to her
father to ask for domestic assistance. The Prophet said: "Shall
I tell you what is better than what you ask? Some words of
praise Angel Gabriel taught me. Say them each thirty-three
times—*subhan Allah, al-hamdu'lillah, Allahu akbar.*"[1] These lita-
nies of praise are still used in the Islamic world and by the Sufis
as a regular practice.

As I worked with this poem, I began to turn from the traditional
story to wonder at the idea of a spiritual gift greater than any
material one. What if instead of someone to help her clean,
cook, and watch the babies, Fatima had asked her Father for
tools to increase her praise and gratitude, inner strength and
direction?

Gift of Prayer

Shyly, she asks her father for some aid.
    Her hands are sore from pulling rope –
        the blisters she will soak
and bind, then grind the grain. She wants a maid.

But what if history reads this wrong? Instead
    she asks him for a wisdom taste
        that Names-of-God may grace
ten-thousand actions and the blessings spread.

Forget the maid. His words can give a hand.
    Each Sacred Name contains a light.
        He's bringing them that night:
subhan Allah, al-hamdu'lillah, and

Allahu akbar – syllables that ring,
    sing open every lock, that key
        to realms that angels see
and hear. The words, the tongue, the shimmering.

A Painting of the Wedding

E kphrastic poetry describes a work of art. This poem was
inspired by an Ottoman Turkish marriage painting from a
fourteenth century manuscript, Siyar-al-Nabi. Similar manuscript
miniatures exist. Following a trail of such references leads
to the Chester Beatty Library in Dublin Castle, Ireland. In this
place, far from the world of Islam, Mustafa Darir's beautiful
miniatures lie tucked away.

It seems that in the last 500 years Fatima's face is not depicted
out of respect for her lofty position in the family of the Prophet.[1]
"White face" shows what is understood to be her "…illumina-
tion and divine grace."[2]

A Painting of the Wedding: Fatima Speaks

Words like *purity*, *haloed* can't excuse how
       father's face and my own are lacking features.

Crowns of flame! We're ignited. Since I'm sightless,
       I just can't understand the why of whiteness.

Blessing ritual? Muhammad's robe is green, his
       hands will join us together. Ali's graced with

physiognomy, hair beneath his turban,
       beard, and eyes and a smile. His mouth can taste the

cake—whatever is shared. I'm blank-faced, burning,
       held inside and concealed. No conversation.

Joy Thief

The early days of exile, the first people of Islam were dressed modestly in earth colors. Wearing jewelry was discouraged. White was the appropriate clothing choice for pilgrimage and still is today. The women did not wish to bring attention to them selves. In contrast, polytheists, who worshiped ancient gods and goddesses used brighter dyes in red and orange colors.

Once Prophet Muhammad made an unusual suggestion to the woman in his community that wearing color was cheerful. His son-in-law, Ali, returned from battle to find his wife, Fatima dressed in something brighter. He complained to Muhammad.

This tale has Sunni and Shia sources. The word "red" is not spoken directly but may be seen as a "cheerful color."

Joy Thief

Red. She wore red. Where is modesty's quiet? He
Just arrived home after days of hard riding,
dismounting—tripped over a pail of boiled flowers
she used to raise blushes in hand-dyed fabric.

A sunny kaleidoscope, landslide, a sweet glide of
crimson spilled. Flame-bursting brass lit the pail next to
that one with cat-calls of copper and orange.
Scarlet? A grimace, that joy thief—her husband—

jaw set and silent, walked off to her father, threw
dust on his head, he said: "Red, she wore red."
Slaughter! The agonized wounded I left there!
Bright shone the blood as it splattered the road-side.

My wife. She reached out to me, red—Allah—red as
the mouth of a jackal. What must a man do for it?
Muhammad held him, then whispered most gently:
I pray that some day you'll be joyful as she is.

Pregnancy

"At the end of my first month of pregnancy, I felt a fever in my womb, and told my father. He called for a pitcher of water, spoke over it, spat into it, and said, Drink. So I drank it and Allah banished what I was feeling."[1] Al-Rawandi, a twelfth century Shia writer, describes Fatima's pregnancy month by month until Husayn was born. "I felt a crawling on my back, like the crawling of ants between the skin and the garment…"[2] It was reported that these were her symptoms. I went on line and typed in pregnancy and the crawling ants and premature labor. I was given a medical condition called ICP. The description "ants," decreased appetite, nausea, related symptoms match those in al-Rawandi's report. It is not surprising that the child, Husayn, was born early, but for an infant to survive birth in Medina at twenty-eight weeks would have been a miracle.

I wanted to have the form reflect this story closely. Poet Grace Schulman writes: "The Sapphic stanza is a form that urges intensity."[3] The pattern of sapphics serves the subject of illness during pregnancy. There is urgency in the *trochaic* syllables, the origin of the word "trochee" is from the Greek word for "running."[4]

PREGNANCY

1 *Thirst, what thirst!* I whispered. *Fevered belly.*
      Bring me water. He signaled, then my father
         prayed, eyes closed and spat in it. Blessing glowed in
               that glass of water.

2 Itch! My back is "crawling like ants." The flow of
      bile is slowed, it's Intra-hepatic Cho-les-
      tasis—fetal stress. One result is stillbirth.
                              May I get through this.

3 He, Husayn-to-be, brings me drunken brilliance.
      Milk is all my appetite's craving. Cups of
      sheep and goat-milk. I'm brimming over, sweetened.
                              Happiness. Weeping.

4 Fed by prayer, the mosque is my home both day and
      night. Right here all versions of increase come with
      Allah's blest best womb-bright companionship, an
                              up-rush of caring.

5 Growing, moving child in my belly lights the
      niche. My womb illuminates like a lantern.
      Did I say how joyful I am? The fifth month.
                              Night shines like day now.

6 Angels touch. Those wings fan my back. I'm sleeping
      while they pray and blow in my face. Angelic
      little dove then flew into my robe and vanished.
                              Ready for birthing.

7 Unexpected labor is quick. *Rejoice! These
      Ones-That-Touch are guardians.* Birth at seven
      Months. He's premature, but Husayn will live. All
                              Praises to Allah!

Fatima Tells of Interruption

Muhammad came to the house of Fatima and Ali to joyfully give them this message—in the middle of the night:

Rise from your sleep and pray during part of the night
as a free offering, and your Sustainer may raise you
to a glorious station..." [1]

[Qur'an 17:79]

This hadith offers a scene of Muhammad encouraging his daughter and her husband to replace sleep with prayer. Imagine her living with Ali and four small children in exhausting poverty. This is the core of the story, but as the poem develops, the shift is to prayer and the repetition of sacred phrases energizing Fatima.

Since the story is clearly about repeated interruption, the ghazal, which goes back to seventh century Arabia, seemed a natural poetic form. This ghazal unfolds with a rhyme scheme and a repeated word—*interruption.*

FATIMA TELLS OF INTERRUPTION

Night covers me, then laughs, issues its interruptions.
I'm jostled by, uncovered by intrusion, interruption.

My prayers slide off with deep fatigue. I wake to
father's knock. He has renewed his interruption.

See how he smiles: *a people pray!* Late night prayers,
he means, high in a holy mood of interruption!

I kiss his cheek as 'Ali openly remarks: *If God
wishes us to wake, we wake* (an argued interruption).

Our children stir, but then my train of thought
pulls sacred words, and moves, occluding interruption.

As if an eagerness filled everything, I'm held in timeless
locomotion's joy, oh gratitude—no interruption.

While She Sleeps

It was a hot day. Umm Ayman looked in the window and saw Fatima asleep, with the millstone spinning, the cradle holding Husayn rocking itself, and a hand raised in praise. She went to the Prophet and told him what she saw. She asked him, "Who was grinding, rocking, praising?" He laughed and told her the names of three angels.[1]

Husayn holds the tender place in the story, as the son constantly remembered in Shia history, assassinated decades later in the massacre at Karbala. Umm Ayman was the servant of Amina, mother of the Prophet. She assisted in the birth of Muhammad and years later—his children. She was the rock of the family.

WHILE SHE SLEEPS

One grinds. One praises God. One rocks Husayn.
Uplifted gesture in the air—what's this?

Two angels brought by Gabriel—one mills
the grain for Fatima, one gestures praise.

You see it and you don't. Not flesh and blood,
nor anything like that. Transparent hands.

Who rocks Husayn? What fingertips can nudge
The cradle? In the room his mother sleeps,

exhausted, fasting, ripe for angel aid.
Her grindstone turns, as if it were a top

and bread could make itself. *Who rocks Husayn?*
A touch so light, the child smiles in his sleep.

The outside world is still, the stems of thoughts
curl tucked inside, while Gabriel bends down

to stroke his cheek, his heart-shaped face. Don't ask
Who rocks Husayn, that little cup of love.

The Best of Us

By God, daughter of Khadija, the only thing you see is that your mother is favored among us..."[1] These words are shouted at Fatima by Aisha, Muhammad's wife.

Aisha the young wife of Muhammad was the daughter of his close companion, Abu Bakr. She was the most clever and outspoken of the Prophet's wives. Continual mention of Muhammad's first wife, Khadija, enraged Aisha. Here, she speaks up for herself and Fatima witnesses the wrath.

Shia stories do not look kindly on Aisha. Sunni historians view her more positively, and offer over two-thousand hadith traditions she gathered from her years in Medina.

THE BEST OF US

Aisha raved at Fatima, flung epithets.
Her words were cruel, a needless vicious snake,
a sudden strike, bright venom meant to ache,
break up the family trust that lets bereft
hands reach for one another, sad thoughts drift
in safety here. Khadija's memory provoked
Aisha's jealousy. So Fatima spoke
to her with firmness, ignored the twist, the hiss.
Muhammad did that too. It made her mad.
Is she the best of us? Aisha burned.
She's dead! Bare truth was flung but then it turned
on her. She felt the shock, stunned and word-clad,

alone in what she'd said, could not un-say
watched Fatima rise, turn and walk away.

Request: a pantoum

After Khadija's death, Muhammad married several women, mostly for political alliances or to care for widows of his friends. Aisha was considered to be his favorite wife. Visitors and members of the community in Medina would wait until it was her day to be with the Prophet, then they would visit him in her room and make offerings. This became a point of irritation to the other wives. "Then they (the wives) called Fatima, and sent her to the Messenger of Allah to say: 'Your wives ask you for fairness regarding (Aisha) the daughter of Abu Bakr.' "[1]

This hadith expresses the relationship between the two leading women in the community. Fatima is caught between her father and the wives, with Aisha prevailing. Because this theme was underlying and repetitive, obsessive even—the "pantoum" poetry form can add to the richness of this view of life in a harem.

REQUEST: A PANTOUM

The wives make a reques*t:*
Since gifts are offered on *her* day,
Find out: Aisha ranks as best?
Seems fairness was tossed away.

Since gifts are offered on *her* day,
good will is wearing thin.
Seems FAIRNESS was tossed away,
one shouts, to fill me in.

Good will is wearing thin,
I, Fatima, am at her door,
she nods to let me in.
I'm their ambassador.

I, Fatima, am at her door,
ask father: *Is it fair?*
I'm their ambassador!
He smiles, she gives a stare.

Ask father: *Is it fair?*
Do you love what I love?
he smiles. She gives a stare.
Oh, yes! They're hand in glove.

Do you love what I love?
He tells me: *love this woman*
Oh, yes! They're hand in glove.
I bite my tongue. Reply? I've none.

He tells me: *love this woman*
with father—I'm aligned.
I bite my tongue. Reply? I've none.
Seems neutral ground is hard to find.

With father—I'm aligned.
Found out: Aisha ranks as best?
Seems neutral ground is hard to find
when wives make a request.

Muhammad's Wounds

The word *Islam* is associated with "the inner state that causes the feeling of peaceful surrender to the protection, safety, and healing of the Divine."[1]

Muhammad refused to fight in the early part of his life. After he moved to Medina in 622 CE, his enemies in Mecca pursued him and his followers with well-armed men. Revelation spoke through him giving permission to *fight, when attacked, for those who have been oppressed...*[Q. 22:39].[2] At one such battle he nearly lost his life.

I'm referring to the Battle of Uhud, 625 CE. Fatima is credited with going to him on the battlefield and dealing boldly and efficiently with the injury. The Shia and Sunni commentators relay the same story.

MUHAMMAD'S WOUNDS

They found a gorge, a hidden place and dragged him there.
He bled, near death. Unconscious. Whispers. Prayers.

Crushed helmet, teeth he lost or didn't lose. Ali
Brought water in a shield. She washed his face.

She burned straw matting, packed it tightly in the wound—
he bled, chain mail embedded in his cheek.

Alive because the enemy read certain death
in such a bloody sight. Alive because

 (while pagan women yelled and mutilated corpses
on the hill) she set warm ash against his flesh,

his face, the throbbing blood, her hand, the bandage—straw.
She held him in, life's tourniquet. Both hands.

Pressed with her life, her every part aligned until
child-like, his pulse slowed, quieted—he'd live.

Hamza: 'Amm al-Kabir

F atima's great uncle Hamza was killed in the Battle of Ubud, and buried in the Martyr's Graveyard. *'amm al-kabir* translates in Arabic, *uncle of your father*. *Kabir* means incomparable greatness. This describes Hamza ibn Abdul-Mutyalib well. He was an exceptional warrior and protector. Fatima loved him and grieved deeply for him. It is said she made prayer beads from the dirt and her tears. [1] She would have repeated God's name (*tasbih*) with each clay bead over and over.

HAMZA: 'AMM AL-KABIR

kneeling at your grave
my tears made the mud
my hands squeezed
    'amm al-kabir

you kept us safe
with your own life
knew me for who I am
    'amm al-kabir

there's nothing left of you
but this, my *tasbih*
pressed pearls of clay
    'amm al-kabir

beads from that earth
move through my hand
string tied with your name
    'amm al-kabir

She Cleans the Swords

Muhammad is a sharp sword, drawn from its sheath
The whole world is illuminated by his divine light. [1]

In the earthy tradition of the Sunni commentators, it is reported that after the battle of Uhud, Fatima was given the swords her father and husband had used, with their words: "Wash the blood off this..." [2]

The Topkapi Museum in Istanbul displays the two swords mentioned in the poem. One is the sword named *Al-'Abd*, Muhammad used at the Battle of Uhud, and cleaned by Fatima in this poem. It is said that his followers touched it as part of the demonstration of fealty to him.

The sword, in the seventh century, was a tool of survival, a companion of life and death on the battlefield, and the protecting weapon of a man's family, his people.

thawb – an blouse-like garment worn over a long loose skirt, pronounced, *toe-b.*

54

SHE CLEANS THE SWORDS

Praying, Fatima whispers: "Allah!" pouring
water over the sticky metal; washing
scrubbing, watching the red run pale. Protection—
loss. A sob. She hears infant Hasan's cries for
her, his screams. She sees slaughter. Driven blades of
pain. While milk wets her thawb, she holds the edge.
Swords are sharper than any cutting tool. Here's
blood from men newly dead, her milk, her tears, and
under each ruddy fingernail—a darkness.

Part Three

The Hungry Years

The Hungry Years

Ibn Sa'd, a prominent Sunni source writes: "Ali said, 'I married Fatima when I did not have a bed except a ram skin. We slept on it at night and fed the camel on it.'"[1] A Shia historian tells of those hungry years that once Fatima's children were sick and there was no food in the house. Ali went to a Jewish neighbor who said, "Here's barley and a bag of sheep's wool in exchange for spinning the wool into yarn." So Fatima ground the barley and made bread so they could eat, then spun the wool.[2]

For most of the years in Mecca, her family was prosperous. But exile offered few opportunities for ease. There was a brief reprieve after 628 CE, when the community received food and service from the conquered city of Khybar. That was short lived, ending four years later, after Muhammad's death.

THE HUNGRY YEARS

Fatima squats to wash their clothes.
No table, tablecloth, no chairs.
The food may be served on woven-wool,
placed in the center of the floor.

There are no fine utensils, plates
for *kusa* squash, her father's treat. [3]
She owns no carpet, hammock, desk,
or windows set in glass, wood screens.

Inside her house, rock geckos dart
through gaps. A cautious cat protects
the grain, sleeping near the grinding stone,
the borrowed spinning wheel, two jugs.

a lamp and oil, a mattress, two—
cloth stuffed with green palm fronds, and sewn.
No book. She wasn't taught to read
in Mecca before the hungry years.

When young, she'd sucked on oranges, fruits
from Syria, touched creamy pearls,
an ivory clasp, brocaded silk,
and gold; gripped tight her mother's hand.

These are the days of barley broth.
She has one small reflective mirror
Her fingers stroke the surface shine,
small habit from that other time.

Camera Obscura

My experience in a hotel coincided with research I was doing on the moment in Fatima's life that seemed to rock her marriage. The incident is as follows: Ali asked the daughter of Abu Jahl (an enemy from Mecca) to be his second wife, then appealed to Muhammad for his council, "'Can you give me advice what to do?' Muhammad answered, 'No. Fatima is from my flesh, and I don't want her to be unhappy.' Then Ali said: 'I'm not going to do anything she dislikes.'"[1]

This is one of the many hadith that came about in the Umayyad era (founded by Muawiyah 661 CE), seeking to cast a shadow on Ali. Whether this happened or not, it is frequently mentioned, so I am putting it in as a window into their married life.

The definition of *Camera Obscura* is, a darkened chamber in which the real image of an object is received through a small opening or lens and focused in natural color onto a facing surface, rather than recorded on a film or plate.

CAMERA OBSCURA

Fatima dreams the sun in her hands restores those who call to her. She wakes to Ali's voice trying to tell her something. She sits up. I'm in a hotel in Phoenix, my mind holding the ashes, warm ashes of Fatima's story, as a long freight train, crosses my wall, a blur of boxcars just beyond the fence, passing through, thrown on the wall from a gap in the drapes — dark light dark, dark light dark, wheels on tracks, on tracks. *Camera obscura*: two places at once, two flung-apart centuries. Fatima lifts her hem, the cotton scented with dried orange-peel from Syria, to flee her husband's words: *a second wife*. She'd like a track to glide upon. She runs. She's a night-storm with lightning. The train whistle warns: *it's not safe, not safe anywhere!* Fatima wants to know what gets me out of bed every day, how I live the dark times. I answer her with a word about gratitude, and a line of sacred syllables —light on dark on light now and now and now, motion-picture-like, the same words her father taught her now bless the train, the whistle, the track, the whole sky, the ashes of everything.

Within the Cloak

For many followers of Islam, "the cloak" or *kisa* is a well-known story, marking Fatima and her family as chosen ones, closest to the Prophet. "Allah's Messenger gathered 'Ali, Fatima, Hasan and Husain under his kisa and said, O Allah, you have given, granted, entrusted your blessing, your forgiveness, your mercy, and your satisfaction to Abraham and his family—those who are from me and I am from them, the a*hl al-kisa* (People of the Cloak). Grant your blessings, mercy, forgiveness, and satisfaction to me and to them."[1] One reference describes Angel Gabriel asking Allah permission to join them as the sixth being under the kisa.[2]

The exclusion of the daughters of Fatima from this picture has led me to explore references to see whether Fatima may have been pregnant with a daughter, since we don't know exactly when this occurred. It seems that she might have carried her last child, Umm Kulthum, in that time period.[3]

Historical commentaries state that these five individuals — Prophet Muhammad, Fatima, Ali, Hasan and Husayn are also identified in a larger context as "…the *ahl al-bayt,* the holy household, the closest family of the Prophet."[4]

WITHIN THE CLOAK

He drew his family close,
under the woolen cloak.
His men saw daughter,
husband, children —
how the little boys
sat on his knees. A family
covered with his cloth.

His men imagined
we imagine now
the dream inside that wrap
the wool from Yemen
with the scent of him,

enclosing those he loved,
all five: Ali, the boys
and Fatima, his daughter,
with a daughter in her womb.

A message there for those
who stood in sun and dust
and wind. They heard
the bloodline blessed.

They witnessed this.
The cloak was small,
was never meant to cover all.

Perfect

A woman "who spent many years teaching Muslim girls, records in her memoirs that she had so many Fatimas and Khadijas in her class that she had to number them."[1] That was because, along with Mary, Mother of Jesus, they were considered *perfect*. There are claims that Aisha and Umm Salama, well-loved wives of the Prophet, are ranked highly, as well.

The American scholar, Denise A. Spellberg, addresses the debates as to who among the wives and daughters is first in rank. Egyptian historian Suyati writes: "Muhammad said to Ali: your wife is the first among Muslims and the most knowledgeable… like Mary was among Christians."[2]

PERFECT

Fatima, are you as peerless as she is?
Exemplary women. Aisha's been named so.
Preeminence links them to father and husband.

Now add Umm Salama. Which wife ranks higher?
Say it— Khadija's placed over Aisha,
but does Khadija give help interceding, like

Mary the mother of Jesus—and Fatima?
Both, if not virgins, are seen so by followers,
people who reify, glorify *perfect*.

Safiyya's Friendship

Safiyya, the Jewish wife of the general of the city of Khaybar had a dream of being with Prophet Muhammad. After the fall of Khaybar and the death of her husband in battle, she shared her dream with the Prophet. Before he returned home they married. [1]

The other wives, especially Hafsa were cruel to Safiyya, so Muhammad asked Fatima to befriend her. Ibn Sa'd notes that Safiyya gave Fatima a pair of gold earrings.[2] This shows a strong link between Fatima and the young Jewish wife, a prey to jealousy. A Moroccan Qadiri Sufi told me tradition says that Safiyya taught those women in the community who wished to understand the ancient religion of the Old Testament, with its stories in the Qur'an.

The story of the earrings contains a pun in Arabic. The root Arabic word d-h-b with a long vowel means GO, while with the short vowel it means GOLD. (*dhahaaba* – go; *dhahaba* – gold).

Hafsa, married to Muhammad was young, and known to be a troublemaker.

Safiyya's Friendship

Those words can hurt, so father had a plan.
He asked my help. *You be her friend.* I nod.
Oh yes! It's yes with him and yes with God.
I told myself —take soup, stop by, and man-
age talk, or offer sympathy, then leave.
She spoke of badgering – one wife or two.
Yes, Hafsa's witty, coarse and rude. I'm new.
She's jealous of most everyone, believe
me! Puns about my jewels and Jews since gold
and go *are twins but for the second vowel*
"Her gold departs and so does she —that meddler!"
Surprise gazelles leapt through her words, so droll
I laughed, then laughed again. She faked a scowl.
We hugged. Gold earrings were a gift from her.

Her House

In Shia stories of Fatima's house, angels dwelt on the roof.
Historian, Ibn Kathir writes in contrast: "The apartments of
the Messenger of God were built on the stalks of palm leaves
covered with mud and partly of stones stacked upon one an-
other. The ceilings were all made of palm fronds." [1]

In Medina the mosque and the rooms of the Prophet's wives
were close enough to Fatima's, for him to stop at the door
and repeat words from the Qur'an every morning (and some
nights as well). There, she and Ali and their four children were
squeezed in. The *mihrab* (prayer niche) of Fatima's house was
said to be on the other side of the wall facing Aisha's room.
This lack of privacy would demand patience from everyone. The
other house in Mecca, belonging to Khadija and Muhammad
was large with room for guests, the children, and storage.

One of the lines of the poem speaks of *Khidr,* an immortal, in
ancient stories, who would appear throughout history and was
said to have taught Moses, yet is unnamed in the Qur'an [Q.
18:60–82]. Sufi narratives say that he offers esoteric wisdom
to those he choses. In popular folklore he aids travelers and is a
protector of believers.[2]

The italic lines are direct quotes from Ansari's *Encyclopedia of
Fatima al-Zahra.*[3]

HER HOUSE

The roof of Fatima's house is God's Holy Throne.
Once I could think higher like that, but I forgot how
twilight and daybreak are structural, like breath.

A prayer in her house is equal to a thousand prayers.
I know better than to ask you how you know this:
her windows tremble slightly, even without glass.

Khidr stopped at the house of Fatima after she died.
He lives on the other side of air, in creations of legend—
It's just like him to not leave a trail or exit through a reference.

Armies of angels descend on the throne of Fatima's house!
Beyond what lands there, beyond wings—the roof has a story:
the light touch of feet, the thousand details of the day.

Demolished

Prophet Muhammad lived in this house in Mecca with his wife Khadija for twenty-eight years at the beginning of the seventh century. Fatima and the other daughters were born here. For centuries it was preserved and venerated.

In 1923 a group of *Wahhabis*, a violent puritanical reformist group destroyed the upper part of the house. In 1989 it was carefully excavated, photographed and reburied under sand and cement. There was a lecture on-line, called "The House of Khadija," given at the University of London, May 11, 2000. In that talk, the Director of Excavation says the house was buried because "the house may encourage idolatry," and "the house is regarded as 'a blessing object' attracting who knows what people." [1]

Phase diggers is an archeological term. The diggers in Mecca had to go below the destruction to a *phase* of history 1,193 years before the destruction of the house.

DEMOLISHED

If it were my house, a good house
demolished,

excavated by phase-diggers whispering
exact measurements in Modern Arabic;
scraping with latex fingers at the stub of the doorway

to the children's room, photographed every part—

> photo 6— the room where Fatima was born, where
> her toes flexed and touched the floor each morning

— if it were my house,
I would sit down in the middle of that room
outraged by history's disregard:
my house—destroyed, buried, dug up, reburied—

and call out the names of Fatima al-Zahra and Khadija.

> photo 7—the room with one niche
> facing Jerusalem, the other—Mecca
>   detail: the water holder for ablutions

> photos 2 and 5—the family dwelling seen from above,
> reception room, prayer room, master bed room,
> children's room, storage, exits—all labeled
>   detail: the bowl of the mill used to grind grain

If it were my house, I would gasp
in the suffocation of sand,
clean sand covering each room on day twenty-one,
the heavy cement poured on the fill
to seal it and make a floor for city storage.

They say the house may encourage idolatry.
They say the house may attract "who knows what people."
They say "a blessing object," as if it were a curse.

If this were my house—the house
where Angel Gabriel appeared, each room

revered long before it was photographed,
I would sit down in the middle of history's disregard
and shout the names—Gabriel and Muhammad,
Khadija and Fatima with a yell bright as blood.

Part Four

Fruit of the Heart

Scent

Prophet Muhammad's wives asked him, "Why do you like Fatima so much?" He replied: "Fatima smells like the scent of paradise. The smell of the prophets is quince, of the *houris* is myrtle, and of the angels is rose. Fatima has the smell of quince, myrtle, and rose.[1]

These beautiful words were said by God's Messenger: "God has made dear to me from your world women and fragrance, and the joy of my eyes is in prayer."

قد جعل الله لي من عالمكم نساء و عطور عزيزة،
و بهجة قلبي هي في الصلاة

Annemarie Schimmel states: "this hadith allows us a glimpse into the twofold function of the Prophet, who knew how to combine this world and the next and… how to sanctify both."[2]

The *houri* – a female heavenly being known for large eyes, like a young gazelle.

SCENT

for Z & T

Three kinds of beautiful,
the best of heaven; blurred
devotion's details meet
Muhammad's love of
Women, prayer and
the perfumes-of-existence…
and the whole world's
neighborhood smells sweet.

Inhaling *Quince*—
urgent as sunrise,
honeyed tonic, golden;
seeded and re-seeded
by love-struck words
in each Revelation.

Myrtle: will grow
only if a woman plants it.
Let's say, Adam
carried the flowers
from paradise to soothe
the grief of expulsion.
Let's say, Eve
dug in the roots,
propagated, cultivated.

Rose: linked to the transparency
of angels, their wings. Washing
with rosewater, we may
become reflective, angelic.

Now introduce the smell
of goats and sweat,
of camel-dung, piss and dust:
seventh century stink.

Cover it with the kiss
of fragrance that is Fatima;
that smell of
Quince, Myrtle, and *Rose*—
all at once.

Muhammad's Death

Muhammad died with his head on the lap of his wife Aisha. During his illness Muhammad told Fatima he would not recover, and she would die soon after him. In the poem she is sitting in the room witnessing his final moments.

Everything would change for Fatima and the world of Islam—as if the sun had ceased to rise. The vehicle for Allah's Message, the man present in all his humanness, compassion, mercy and strength, the one who held the community together—Muhammad would be gone.

Harn is coarse linen.

MUHAMMAD'S DEATH

On this sad night in harn of hush and cling,
his head's un-liftable, life-force expelling.
Aisha's lap, his sweat her tears; a wing
or blink – as quick as that it comes – farewell.
The mood is grave, birds cry, and shadows veil
the sun. It sets, hands shield candle's glow here.
His words come back to me – *My health will fail.*
I groan to see my father swoon and strewn here.
So soon? Crouched in that room, my heart's opaque.
His light, such light! I'm here. I watch him die.
At thought of leaving him I start to shake.
I watch him die. Allah, I watch him die!
The scribes of history grappled with this night
But none has told the moon's astounding light.

Blue Date Cake

Ten days after Muhammad's death, Ali met Salman al-Farsi, a close family friend and follower of the Prophet. Ali told him Fatima had received a gift from Heavenly Beings that she wished to share with him, so he went to her house. She mentioned how the houris had brought a blue date cake because of her great sorrow, and that they spoke his name.

The moment my friend translated this story from Arabic at the table in his living room in Jordan, I knew I had a poem. I pictured three heavenly beings at her door. Her father was dead. Most historians went on and on about her constant inconsolable weeping. That was what was expected of her. A time like that is full of contradictions. She needed to explain to her four children—all under ten years old—what happened to their grandfather, and she needed to care for herself. She would rely on her husband and friends as well as her own internal life to strengthen her. This Shia hadith illustrates heaven's gifts.

Dar as-Salam – the Abode of Peace.

BLUE DATE CAKE

for Marilyn Hacker

The door opened. I lay in tears alone.
Three women stepped inside. They weren't from here.
I asked them in.
Where have you been, O Eyes-of-Heaven's Own?
One answered: *Paradise! And we're*
sent here by God with cake to ease death's pain.

Your father—You are longing for him. We know.
Salman, I asked their names. They mentioned yours
and gifted us
with blue date cake fragrant as musk, and oh,
one bite! I felt the grief reverse.
I ate and in that rare deliciousness

I slipped right out of time. Before the taste
and peaceful scent of *Dar as-Salam* arrived,
erosive streams
of loss tore through my life. I had misplaced
my father's love-words. They revived.
One seed opened inside and sweetened me.

The Sermon

Imagine this today—a *woman* gives a sermon at a mosque. Yet here is "...Fatima, 'a truth teller, a witness.' The essence of Fatima's role... is to respond, and thus she is at her most important when her response is clear and articulate."[1] In her speech in the mosque of Medina after Muhammad's death, she protests the wrongs done by the Muslim community. She is associated here and elsewhere with "miraculous knowledge of what is to come."[2]

I had never heard or read about Fatima's Sermon. The Sunni historians don't mention it. One day, nearly a decade ago, I asked to speak to my Iranian friend and scholar, Dr. Shah Nazar Seyed Ali Kianfar about the family of the Prophet. He had just translated Fatima's *Speech at the Mosque*, he told me. In Iran it is well known. I was stunned. That is how I began to learn Fatima's story is not the same everywhere. What follows is my interpretation.

Al-barzakh is an interface between the physical and spiritual world.

THE SERMON

She speaks in the mosque.
She hears her voice as an echo
of what he used to say,
a moon-like reflection.
She hears him

inside her warming
her chest, her tongue.
She doesn't have to
think about the words.
The heat of
the-sun-that-is-him
dries her tears.
She's standing
in front of everyone,
reminding them
of their forgotten loyalty,
Revelation's teaching,
the truth of Prophecy.
She foresees the outcome—
betrayals, treachery, injustice.
Her voice holds him now.
Sunset will come
and the stars vanish
at dawn. You know
those moments when
the *barzakh,* between
heaven and earth
dissolves, and that
dazzling rawness
makes it impossible
for all but a sweet
child or two, and those
who hold the ancient truths
to remember history,
to remember anything.

One Reason

Abu Bakr was the first Caliph After Muhammad's death. There was no precedent to guide his decision-making, although he intended to follow Muhammad's wishes. Muhammad had been the only leader this community had known. The Caliph took away Fatima's patrimony—palm orchards known as *Fadak*. Fatima's address to the community at the mosque known as "the sermon" asked him to reconsider his decision.

The speech is lengthy. It speaks to how the followers have fallen off the path that Muhammad indicated by his example and teachings. In an interesting twist, the wives—but not Fatima's family were supported by the community. In the decades that followed, this legal judgment was overturned, then reinstated then overturned over and over.

Expropriation is a legal term that means to take possession of, especially for public use by the right of eminent domain; to dispossess a person of ownership.

ONE REASON

The judgment's wrong. I want his promise kept.
It's meant for us—Fadak—the land,
our property, the planned
support in daily life, provisions swept

away. Expropriation steals. Retract
your words. Would he have wanted us
to beg for alms? Breadless?
His words: *they can't inherit* —inexact.

The orchards give us livelihood. Permit
Inheritance, o Holder of
Islam. This gift with love
meant for my family. Let us benefit.

Ali Says Goodbye

Just before Prophet Muhammad died, he predicted Fatima would be the first to join him. Some say she died of heartbreak, grief and illness during August, 632 CE, just ten weeks after her father.

She left behind her husband, Ali, who was also her cousin on her father's side. He was often called Abu'l-Hasan, which translates "father of Hasan," the firstborn. Ali had grown up in Muhammad's household, so he'd known his wife since she was a child. In the years of conflict he would ride into battle with Muhammad, and was known as a great warrior. When he would despair or become frustrated or grief-stricken he would throw dust on his head, so Muhammad nicknamed him, "Father of Dust." Since his death the Shia venerate him.

The *ghaf* tree grows in the desert with long, fast-growing roots.

ALI SAYS GOODBYE

I am the voice that begs Fatima not to die
I am the *ghaf* tree that pleads with the earth,
    'Hold fast my roots'
I am the sword she cleaned, the lips she kissed
I am the face she held with rinsed hands
I am the head nodding, yes
I am her private night burial
I am the tears spilled for her
I am her husband, Abu'l-Hasan
I am her cousin
I am her feet as she stands for justice
Only she will have me—I am the prey of the lioness

She is a purse of gold, a crown of Certainty
I am the father of dust.

Letters of Love

S hia historians offer this elegant description of Fatima's last
moments: Bilal, the man who recited the call to prayer in
the first years of Islam, said that Fatima sighed whenever she
repeated: "Muhammad is the Messenger of God." At the end
of her life she was saying these words when she shuddered
and exhaled. That was her final breath.[1] In this mystical version
of her death, the phrase, *Muhammadan rasul Allah,* carries his
daughter to paradise.

The phrase lives in the hearts and on the breath of those who
say it, repeated by a billion Muslims each time they pray. It is a
connection to the Messenger and what he brought to Arabia in
the seventh century—God's Message, the Qur'an.

The quote in line five is from The Sufi, Hazrat Inayat Khan who
writes: "...the *Rasul* (Messenger) is the one who represents
God's perfection through human limitation." [2]

Muhammadan rasul Allah

Letters of Love

for Annie Finch.

Houris call to her spirit, signal nightfall.
Firm, encompassing hands untie her life; she

exhales Arabic. Dazzling repetition
lifts: *Muhammadan rasul Allah* echos
"God's perfection through human limitation."

On these letters of love she can fly to heaven.

Glory

Fatima is described in elaborate detail, in Shia history, crossing the bridge to paradise. "On the Day of Resurrection, a herald will call from the middle of the throne: 'O people of the Resurrection, lower your gaze, for Fatima the daughter of Muhammad is crossing.'"[1]

The dactylic meter can be described as "a magnetic and insistent rhythm," and like a "many-sounding sea."[2] Dactylics are used here to inscribe the moment a great heavenly camel—accompanied by horses—bears the daughter of God's Messenger high above the fires of hell to the Throne Room in the heart of Paradise.

GLORY

Fatima rides with the emerald houris,
maidens—immortals with transcendent eyes.
High on that she-camel known as al-Adba,

dressed in a thousand sheer garments of heaven,
with beautiful greetings inscribed on each hem.
Five thousand angels go with her as escort

on sapphire horses with pearls in their manes,
joining this liminal moment of glory:
she's crossing death's bridge, but it's wide as a hair.

Gabriel guides her into God's throne room.
Here, like a bride, she is light-crowned and perfect,
while star-marked galaxies gleam in her hair.

She's known as the doorway to life-everlasting.
Calling and crying for help, people beg her:
Please help us, lift us right over the gap.

Replaced

M uhammad thought of his grandsons as "sons." It is mentioned in hadith how delighted he was with them, how he carried them about, and let them climb on him. In 632 CE the young boys lost both grandfather and mother, Fatima. Imam Ali became ruler and guide in 656 CE.

Hasan, Fatima's first son became Imam when Ali was assassinated in 661 CE. He was soon overwhelmed by Muawiyah, a power-hungry leader who founded the Umayyid dynasty. Hasan, a man of a peaceful nature saw no way to continue in the face of opposition. He abdicated and retired to Medina.

REPLACED

I
Hasan, the boy who rode Muhammad's shoulders,
on the wing of things,
who climbed grandfather's back as he knelt at the mosque.
"O, Hasan," Muhammad said, "you are like me in manner,
appearance, character."[1]

II
Hasan replaced his father, Ali, who ruled after three caliphs.
He filled the mosque, the street and more:

> "I am Hasan, son of Muhammad.
> I am the shining lamp…"
> Most Muslims pledged their loyalty to him.
> He spoke Qur'an:
> "Love those who are near and love your fellow man.[2]

III
Fatima's son, Imam Hasan,
now faced Muawiyah, most bitter rival,
who pushed him out and plotted with Ja'da, his wife.
Wife and foe arranged a poisoned meal.

She fed Hasan the food of death.

> The work of shadow-hands eclipsed
> The brightened light—
> That fool stepped up to rule… and then another.

IV
The undercurrent tugs at what it touches—rocks and roots.
Dark waters pour through everything,
the climate of love, replaced.

Moon

The "moon of grief" is the crescent that marks the Islamic New Year and the first ten days of of the month of mourning (Muharram) for the Shia. On the tenth day, known as *Ashura*, Sunni Muslims fast, and the Shia acknowledge the death of Fatima's second son, Husayn and other companions at Karbala on the shore of the Euphrates in 680 CE.

The sights and sounds of *Ashura* are gripping: a towering hand that represents the *ahl al-bayt,* a riderless white horse, an empty saddle, women weeping, men, four abreast—all dressed in black. "Ya Husayn," the men and women beat their chests and chant. "This is a ritual filled with symbolism and passion." [1]

The *ahl al-bayt* – the holy household, descendants of the Prophet with Fatima and Ali.

MOON

Alas! Mourning has begun.
Alas! The moon of grief has
shown her face. [2]

When the night comes
the Euphrates drifting
towards Karbala,

the land dark,
pockmarked by tears
crisscrossed by boot-prints,

a crescent moon
above blood glass,
a shattered shrine.

The sky we look upon is black.
We stumble, fall through the millennia,

I call your name, *Husayn.*
I speak for all who mourn.

Winter Landscape

For the story of Fatima, her son Husayn's death goes beyond space and time. It is the anchor of pain in the vast Shia family—this tragic demise. When I began my work on Fatima a wise friend and scholar, Cemâlnur Sargut said to me, "... with the loss of your son you have permission to do this work."

This poem began in a Wyoming winter, as I sat on the carpet, surrounded by photos of my son, Solomon, who had died just over a year before, and the two losses became one.

WINTER LANDSCAPE

for Solomon

Fatima has photos of
her son, Husayn, spread out on the floor
where she sits. There's one of him with
his arm around her.

They smile the same smile.

Next to that is the small
shot of Husayn and his brother on
Qaswa. Ali holds the camel.
In close-up, he looks

like he might be saying — Ooooo!

The 8 x 10 shows them
together on the sand at sunset. He is
wearing a hat with his sunglasses
folded in his hand.

His hands, her hands, share
a pattern of fingers, his stronger.

Fatima watches a winter
landscape, the chill wrapped
around her like a blanket. An angel
insists on telling her future. The world
she knows will tilt, and the one who

—like the prophet Solomon — brings joy

and wisdom will be gone. She replaces
the dark disturbance-in-her-mind
with a photo of him: wide grin,

gap between his front teeth.

Last Light Breaking

...all humbling darkness
Tells with silence the last light breaking
And the still hour
Is come of the sea tumbling in harness...[1]

This poem by Dylan Thomas was the ladder I used to climb down into a description of Karbala, the place Fatima's youngest son Husayn was martyred. What is grief, with its continual qualities? How does us carry us? What signs of life do we grasp so as not to become merged with death? How do we embrace the paradox of refusal to mourn and the need to feel? I was determined to keep symbols of a physical connection as Thomas does—*the sea tumbling in harness*. In my poem the final lines—*blood, soil, feet, milk, goats* serve to tie the loss of a child—Fatima's, mine—to every-day life.

The terrible massacre at Karbala is the heart of Islamic tragedy, and the ongoing jagged wound within Shia Islam. "Much of Shi'ism is about memory and commemoration—about the need to remember those who came before, how they lived and how they died... to not forget the possibility of living a heroic life." [2]

Regarding Husayn's demise at Karbala, " The *Qawwalis* (Sufi musicians) are more favorably disposed to view death as victory, a union with God, than to view death as an event to be mourned"[3]

Allah-hu – sacred phrase referring to God.

Last Light Breaking, the Death of Husayn

Tonight this moon-splashed life is milk made gray by tears.
Grief wants it all—what's here and then what's gone.

I share with you, the dirge, the wind that sings in bone.
Etched there inside my eyelid is his look.

The tragic and divine, they twine like serpent kin.
Pain cuts, drives deep. I call on *Allah-hu*.

O, Fatima, pale mother of Husayn, such loss!
This storyteller leans toward Prophet's kin.

The blood from soil in Karbala has stained our feet.
Cruel times. The milk of seven goats runs dry.

Shahrbanu and the Royal Fabric

Shahrbanu was daughter of the last pre-Islamic ruler of the Persian Empire. Her connection with Husayn came to be legend in Persia. It was written that around ten years after Muhammad's death she was captured and brought to Medina where Ali rescued her from slavery and arranged for her to marry his son Husayn. Shahrbanu and Husayn became parents of Ali Zayn, who became the fourth Shia Imam.

Marriage between the ancient Iranian monarchy and the family of the Prophet encouraged the adoption of Islam by the Persians. The Iranians wrote Shahrbanu stories, only found in their tradition.[1] However, the tale of this union of families through Ali Zayn holds an important message of peace for the Arabian and Persian people.

SHAHRBANU AND THE ROYAL FABRIC

Ali Zayn, like a single royal prayer cloth
soothes both nations and folds around them gently

after Karbala, Arab stitched to Persian.
Ali Zayn holds the golden thread—weaves back and

forth with silk pulled from Persian fine brocade and
linen, frayed by the years Muhammad wore it.

Two—son-stitched into one: Husayn is pressed with
gold to Shahrbanu, mother, princess, queen of

legends, written with exhaltation. When it's
dark their quilt joins the family, touches, warms them.

Standing Tall

When Fatima's two daughters, Zaynab and Umm Kulthum are mentioned anywhere, it is generally in the aftermath of Karbala. Often, they are not named. There are many thousands of pages on their brother, Husayn, in Arabic. There are stories of Hasan and Husayn, beginning when their grandfather, Muhammad was alive. But for the daughters there are scraps. There is often disagreement as to whom and when they married, time of death, and where each was buried.

When I was in Syria for several weeks in 2003, I dressed like a Syrian Muslim woman, not a tourist. At the shrine of Ibn al-Arabi, and other places, the men I was traveling with blended in easily. I was met with criticism and insistence that I copy local women in behavior and every aspect of prayer. I came to understand that if I stood out, it was a danger to all, so like a nail, I must be flattened like the others.

STANDING TALL

She remains a speaker, though silent;
remains, although invisible, a woman.
—Marilyn Hacker

My daughters are like nails sunk in a board,
when hammered down, they seem to disappear.
Repudiation you can't miss, ignore.

The music in the metal of their names
rings out, indelible, a small bright mark—
just even with the wood's smooth grain. Explain.

Each pays a subtle price should she stand tall,
yet daughters hold the home, each room in place
the roof, the beams, the floor, and every wall.

Lioness labu'a

لبؤة

"F atima is associated with miraculous knowledge of what is to come."[1] Many Shia believe so. Her father's legacy was twisted right after his death. That deeply disturbed her. She came to the struggle for his work empowered by strong women. Khadija's ancestors most likely worshiped the divine mediator, al-'Uzza, one of the primary goddesses in Mecca before Islam. This idea is affirmed by the fact that her great–great grandmother was named 'Atiqa b. 'Abdul 'Uzza. Khadija ran her own business and took care of the family financially. She supported Muhammad's work as God's Messenger. Muhammad's great-grand-mother, Salma, was consulted by his father's family.[2] We know these stories from Sunni hadith.

The lioness stands for all the feminine confidence and power Fatima inherited from both sides of her family. It would follow that the bond between Fatima and her daughters is reflected in the kind of strength and confidence I witnessed in the Muslim Sufi women in North Africa.

Zaynab would have been five when her mother died.
Umma – name given to the Muslim community.

LIONESS LABU'A

I am dying. Listen, daughter.
Now, you're the lioness.
Guard our family. Life is dangerous,
the telling of it in disorder.
Help our people know us and remember.
Strengthen clan and honor.

Hear *Labu'a,* in your trackless habitat,
your mother's fading roar.
Catastrophe and loss are imminent.
Take my speed, my power and my claws.
Use all three wisely. In the Arabian desert,

—deceit and brutal martyrdom
to come—both lions and the *umma,*
those who love the desert and the Prophet
need you as their guardian. I call on
your ferocious passion. Help them to survive.

Over Damascus

Over a decade ago, I visited *The Shrine of Sayyida Zaynab* (granddaughter of Prophet Muhammad) in the suburbs of Damascus. It seemed like the well-in-the-desert for women, a place we could all feel empowered.

Recently, it was under attack twice, caught in the crosshairs of the Syrian conflict. The regime that the terrorists are trying to overthrow is "Alawi." The name comes from "Ali," although they are an independent Muslim group. This is a very important shrine in Damascus. Some opponents of the Syrian Regime would like to demolish it.

Zaynab is the patron saint of the nurses of Syria, because she was at Karbala when her brother, Husayn and many others were killed. She stood up to the tyrant Yazid, as mentioned in this poem, written before the recent attacks.

OVER DAMASCUS: A SONNET

Salaam Great Zaynab, lit at night, shines warm
above the arch below the golden dome.
They say your name is charmed. A honeycomb
against a sting; you face the one who harms.
Yazid-the-tyrant dragged you here and killed
your family. You called him out—"Dark foe!
You bear the burden of blood you shed, and so
your loss comes. God judges!" It was brilliant,
that speech you gave. O mother of the ones
who call, gunfire's here, windows fly apart.
Tomb keeper's dead, grandson held to his heart.
This marble floor is sharp with glass. We summon
you. Please come. Damascus lies here stung and stung
Such pain! *Zaynab*, your name lives on my tongue.

Almost Nothing, With a Beauty All Its Own

There is almost nothing to go on. Umm Kulthum was the second daughter of Fatima and Ali. Was she buried in the Bab Sagher Cemetary in Damascus or the Baqi Cemetary in Medina? Did she die at Karbala or after? Was she married to Caliph Umar or to the young man, Uwn b. Jaffar? Perhaps both. There are few consistent stories of Fatima's youngest daughter.

ALMOST NOTHING, WITH A BEAUTY ALL ITS OWN

I
What Some Muslims Tell:

They talk about her mother boiling goat bones a second time, hauling water, calling brother Hasan, or her other brother. There are sentences, pages about the famous family. The one-year-old girl is never mentioned. Her grandfather dies. The breast that sustained her dries up. The house grows cold as winter. Her mother dies. Death and flies are everywhere. Her sister tries to soothe her, but no one tells that story. Years go by. She's last of four children. She's given in marriage to the sixty-year-old caliph who oversees Islam.[1] She is thirteen.

II
Variations:

History's distracted with anecdotes about her brothers. She is called by her sister's name plus the Arabic word for "the younger."[2] In this variation, after her mother dies she stays at home until her father marries her to a boy her age. Both are close to adulthood. His name and his parents' names are written down. Other stories say she married the Caliph, and after he died—she married the boy. Years go by. She may have died in 662 CE.[2] Her tomb is in Medina, or maybe one of two places in Damascus.

III
Divergent History and Her Name:

By 680 CE, her mother and grandfather fifty years dead, she remains alive through carnage and capture. As this telling goes, she is faced with the murderous tyrant who ordered the massacre of her brother and others. She stands next to her elder sister and yells out a message: "Children of prophets aren't meant to be slaves of the children of bastards and pretenders!"[3] The Ambassador to Byzantium is quoted as saying: "She is majestic, more so than The Queen of Byzantium."[4] He adds a terse comment about her many eloquent poems, none of which survive. Her name is Umm Kulthum, daughter of Fatima. What she left is almost nothing, with a beauty all its own.

This Tree

Every Sufi lineage traces its wisdom through Ali back to Muhammad. On our *Chishti* lineage tree there is not one woman's name—not even Fatima, or valued teachers such as Rabia al-Adawiyya of Basra. The women are found in scholarly books.

Lost, they have been lost—the names of wise women in the family tree. This saddens me because, for me, Sufism is the flower fragrance of mysticism—universally inclusive. In my experience, religion is that which connects the devotee with Divine Unity containing both male and female principles.

Ghaf tree – desert plant with green leaves and a very long root, valued in Arabia.
Hud-hud is a Hoopoe, the bird that brought King Solomon news of Bilqis of Sheba.
Lineage – a line of spiritual successors. The *Chishti* lineage traces its leaders back to Moinuddin Chishti – celebrated Sufi Saint of India, thirteenth century.

THIS TREE

Ancestor *ghaf* tree, giraffe tree, oh swing me
up into your crow-crowded branches. King tree,
shade-easy, a climb as you may tree, bouquet tree—
the tree with a green kiss of leaves in the sun.

Camel and she-calf lie shaded, brocaded
by bird-branches splayed in the shade playing shade
against shade in the gravely sand. Around me
the lineage holders are mounted on twigs with the
Hud-hud, a mayfly, as word swells keep spelling
out names, family names, on each branch as I sit here
while breezes call "Ali," "Husayn," then the chain—
in Arabic, Turkish, in Persian and more.

But where are the she-mystics, Fatima's wise ones?
Invisible. Guides to the green genealogy—
whispers of sisters just nourish us all and
churn family butter from roots of the *ghaf* tree.

In Flight

This was one of those metaphoric poems that nearly wrote itself when I started thinking about Fatima, how she is known as *Umm Abiha*, "the mother of her father," how he and those who invoke her trust what she says and does. *He is pleased*—he tells himself—*to be in her hands.*

IN FLIGHT

for Maeve

Fatima, daughter of Khadija, is a pilot.
She is trustworthy as salt. Her knowledge
demystifies navigational instruments.
She holds a perfect safety record.

The Prophet has a seat in economy class.
the airline lets him ride free. He stretches
and yawns, works the crossword with
a number two pencil. He is looking for
a short word for handlers of history.

He is thinking about the usefulness of an eraser,
the technology of flight. Like Revelation,
a matter of fuel, acceleration, lift.

He contemplates the pilot's job; to crease
a brief diagonal in the sky's fabric
then fly the 747 at 38,000 feet.
Fatima does this. *He is pleased —*
he tells himself—*to be in her hands.*

He taps his eraser on the tray table and pauses,
a four letter word that begins with the letter B —
considers scholars and mangled meanings;
that is, what they made of his work
his life, the Message. Bent or bash won't fit.
Ah: bias.

The Call and Response

I have used the call and response form here as a poetic conver-
sation to contain unexpected lore from the *Encyclopedia Irani-
ca*. Such a conversation seems to me an apt completion for this
group of poems on Fatima al-Zahra. The traditions listed begin
and end with the breaking of food and water vessels. "I hear
the sound of breaking," demonstrates how millions of people
appreciate and feel the blessing and sadness of Fatima and her
family. As she was an echo for her father, I am honored to serve
as an echo for this extraordinary woman and her legacy.   Thank
you, Sayyida Fatima.

The Call and Response

*Whoever pleases Fatima has
pleased God ... Fatima is a part
of me.*

Prophet Muhammad

On the last Wednesday of the solar year, they break
earthenware pots in her honor

I hear the sound of the breaking.

The waters of heaven and earth were part of her dowry—
as salt, jasmine, and the pomegranate.

*O, grain of salt, tinted sky,
           white flower, stem bearing fruit.*

She shines in a host of texts.
No one talks about her quarrels with 'Ali.
All those words are washed away.

I apologize for the rain over fallen tree-trunks of legend.

Her name is sometimes given to girls born on Friday night.
Samanu is a kind of pudding
reputed to have been her favorite dish.

While I twirl my spoon, I say her name.

She guards two of the secret and sacred books
of the Immaculate Ones,

113

two tablets of white pearl and emerald.

From meaning to meaning she comes to us.

She discloses the cavern of the Seven Sleepers,
the rock of Moses which brings forth fresh water.

I taste her prayers in each fresh desert rill.

Fatima is linked to immortal Khidr.
Often, her birthday is often honored as Mother's Day.

Mother of how-this-story-goes,
* her life polishes each child's face.*

She appears as an icon; crowned for Muhammad,
with earrings of diamond or ruby for departed ones.

Hasan! Husayn!   I hear the sound of breaking.

The End

Endnotes:

Preface ◆ *p. xi*

[1] Prophet Muhammad refers to Fatima: "She is from my flesh, the light of my eye and the fruit of my heart." Ansari, *Encyclopedia of Fatima al-Zahra*, 21:327. "The Best of the women among you is Fatima." Suyuti, *Musnad Fatima,* #86. And Bukhari, *Sahih al-Bukhari*, 7: book 62, #157.

[2] Her name is recognized as "Our Lady of Fatima." Three children had a vision of Virgin Mary at a church near the village of Fatima, Portugal in 1917. The town was named after a Moorish princess who bore Fatima's name.

[3] There are different accounts of Fatima's time of death, but this one says she died 75 days after her father. Clohessy, *Fatima,* 153.

[4] Dr. Arthur Buehler, Islamic scholar confirmed and often translated the hadith used in this book, mainly from Arabic sources encouraging strong primary source material.

[5] Definition of the word, "Islam:" was spoken by Imam Bilal Hyde, Sufi and Qur'anic scholar.

[6] http://www.cemalnur.org/contents/detail/cemalnur-sargut-biography/736

Introduction ◆ *p. xv*

[1] See George William Warner, "Tragedy, History, and the Sacred: The *Hujjah* of Fatima al-Zahra," *Journal of Shi'a Islamic Studies*, 4/2/11, 158. For many Muslims, Fatima's heart held the calamities to come, and lives on in each tragedy. This article mentions the angels told her what the future held.

[2] Ansari, *Encyclopedia of Fatima,* 4:12. "The roof of Fatima's house..."

Sacred Names ◆ *p. 2*

[1] Clohessy, *Fatima*. 87-89. In cultures of the Islamic world, there are lists of the "Blessed Names of Fatima al-Zahra." Here is an on-line example: http://www.yanabi.com/index.php?/topic/123730-87-blessed-names-of-sayyidatina-fatima-az-zahra-rady-allahu-anha/

One Morning in Sayfad-din's Kitchen ◆ *p. 4*

Form: hendecasyllabics

Fruit-of-the-Heart: a sonnet ◆ *p. 6*

1 The story of Fatima's birth dates with this version of the fruit and *the Night Journey* is not held by all Muslims (See #4. "Dates"). Historical reference: Clohessy, *Fatima*, 22, 78, 79. Suyuti, *Musnad Fatima*, #110.

Dates ◆ *p. 8*

1 When was Fatima born? There are several versions: "Fatima (was)... born when Quraysh were rebuilding the Ka'ba." (year 605). Ibn Sa'd, *The Women of Madina*, 18. And "Fatima was born when Muhammad was 39 years old, 5 years before Revelation." Tabari, *The History*, 39:66. From another perspective, "The Shia scholar, Majlisi holds that Fatima was born in Mecca... five years after the prophetic call (year 610 CE) and three years after the 'night journey' when the Quraysh were reconstructing the Ka'ba." Clohessy, *Fatima*, 23.

"Fatima Dies at age 18." Ansari, Encyclopedia of Fatima, 2:234. Since Hasan was born in 624, and was 8 when his mother died, in this reference she was 10 when she gave birth.

Stories depicting Mother Khadija's age equate long life and wisdom. As a result, she was spoken of as "older than Muhammad," then 40, or "old" [up to 15 years older]. I believe Khadija's age to be exaggerated. The number 40 is a place mark for a mature, respected person.

Dates and butter were a favorite food for Muhammad. *Anbara Medina:* a type of date known for its sweet taste and healing properties.

The Silver Hand ◆ *p. 10*

Schimmel, *And Muhammad*, p. 19.

Delivery ◆ *p. 12*

1 Wife of Pharaoh (step-mother to Moses) Asiya bint Muzahim, is a model of faith. She is mentioned in the Qur'an [Q: 28:9, 66: 11].

2 Clohessy, *Fatima*, 84, 85. Sources Majlisi, (Shia), Tabari (Sunni). This is a Syrian teaching story, with Khadija age fifty, although realistically Khadija was younger. Ibn Sa'd, *The Women,* " 8:13 relates that Fatima was born "...while the Quraysh were re-building the Ka'ba. That was five years before prophet-hood." Tabari, *The History*, 9: 128 agrees. This sets the time table back a decade, putting Fatima into a life of privilege for the first seven or so years of her life, then as she grew

117

into adolescence, her family life became difficult. Some Arab traditions name these "The Women of the Book" present at her birth.

3 Kahn, *Untold*, 153, fn 11.

Ghazal ◆ *p. 14*

1 "A man of the Quraysh…brought a sheep's entrails, which he then threw over my head while I was prostrate in prayer. Fatima came and washed it off my head." This was spoken by Prophet Muhammad. Most of the sources say, "camel" not "sheep." See Ibn Kathir, *The Life*, 2:318. Bukhari, *Sahih*, 1, book 4, #241, and 4, book 52, #185, fn 5.

2 Kahn, *Untold*, 9. *Hilm* from the Arabic root *hlm*, refers to dreaminess, tenderness and nurture that is an antidote for anger.

Form: ghazal.

Planned Famine: Mecca, around the year 617 ◆ *p. 16*

Aslan, *No god but God*, 46.

Lings, *Muhammad*, 89.

Ansari, *Encyclopedia of Fatima*, 21:396. Khadija on her deathbed says that the opposing Qurayshi women oppress Fatima (during the famine) and do not allow her to do anything.

Form: hendecasyllabics.

Going On ◆ *p. 18*

See Tuysirkani, *al-Musnad Fatimat*, #136:253.

Ansari, *Encyclopedia of Fatima*, 21:389, 390, 397.

Form: sapphics.

Shine ◆ *p. 20*

Clohessy, *Fatima*, 95, fn 312, (Ibn Babuya].

Form: One-sentence sonnet, after Robert Frost, "The Silken Tent."

The Jinn ◆ *p. 22*

1 Jinn are frequently mentioned in the *Qur'an* and taken seriously in most Islamic cultures.

2 Quote: Ansari, *Encyclopedia of Fatima*, 17: 528.

3 When Muhammad was on Mt. Hira, Gabriel squeezed him and forced him to recite the first words of Revelation. [Q. 96:1-5]. His fear was that he was just possessed by jinn.

Form: dactylic tetrameter.

Wild Honey of *Adab* ✦ *p. 26*

[1] Kabbani, *Encyclopedia*, 16. Here is the quote about Fatima. Aisha related: "She never saw anyone more like God's Messenger in respect to gravity, calm deportment, pleasant disposition, and speech than Fatima. When Fatima went to visit the Prophet, he stood up to welcome her, took her by the hand, kissed her and made her sit where he was sitting. When he went in to visit her she got up to welcome him, took him by the hand, kissed him, and made him sit where she was sitting." Same quote in Clohessy, *Fatima*, 46.

In contrast, Fatima and Aisha from a Shia perspective, see poems in this book: "The Best of Us," p. 47. "Request," and p. 49. "Perfect", p. 65.

Escape into Exile ✦ *p. 28*

[1] Ansari, *Encyclopedia of Fatima*, 2:221. The Prophet sent Ali a note saying to arrange for the three Fatimas— including Ali's mother and a cousin— to assemble at night and travel with him to Medina. Most accounts don't name Ali as the one to bring Fatima and the women in the family to Medina.
Red-Legged-Clump-Wing is an ostrich in pre-Islamic poetry. Sells, *Desert Tracings*, 5.
Night & Horses & the Desert, edited by Robert Irwin, introduction, ix, x. Here is information on the desert view of the ostrich.
[2] Ibn Kathir, *The Life of the Prophet*, 2:184. Aisha tells a different version of how Fatima and her sister left, in Tabari, *The History*, 39: 171-172.
Form: blank verse with variations.

Remedy For Fire ✦ *p. 30*

[1] Clohessy, *Fatima*, 90. fn 288 (Majlisi): The Messenger of God said: "I called my daughter Fatima because God, powerful and lofty, has separated her and separated those who love her from the fire."
[2] Ibid., 184. "...cling to the hem of her cloak..."
Form: hendecasyllabics.

Inscribed in Light ✦ *p. 32*

[1] Fatima's high status and title: Suyuti, *Musnad Fatima*, #75, #87. "Fatima is the Queen of Heaven." And Osman, *Female Personalities*, 166. Clohessy, *Fatima*, 3, describes her. Clohessy mentions in fn 4. Hilali, *Kitab Sulaym b. Qays*. "This is held by scholars to be the oldest

surviving Shia text...before 622."

2 Ibid., 55. Her name is written on God's throne: fn 180 (primary source: Ibn Babuya al-Saduq).

3 Ibid., 179. "Afran the Jinn saw Iblis, the fallen angel pleading with God to take him from the fire to be with Fatima and her family. This angel saw her name on God's throne seven thousand years before God created Adam."

Gift of Prayer ◆ *p. 34*
1 Quote from several sources, all Sunni: Ibn Sa'd, *The Women,* 17-19. Bukhari, *Sahih,* 4, book 53, #344, and also 8, book 75, #330. Form: rhyming iambic quatrains. After A.E. Stallings: "Empty Icon Frame."

A Painting of the Wedding ◆ *p. 36*
The miniature: "Muhammad joins the Hands of Ali and Fatima." Turkish MS 419, folio 24b, from *Siyar-al-Nabi* by Darir, 1398 CE, in the Chester Beatty Library, Dublin.

Clohessy, *Fatima,* 21. "...according to the Sunni scholars... (Fatima and Ali) were nineteen or twenty at this time."

Tabari, *The History,* 39:167, "Ali married Fatima... five months after the Prophet's arrival in Medina. She was then 18 years old." Both Fatima and her father have their heads completely covered, edged with flaming halos. Ali is wearing a green turban and his face is visible. Two angels hold lit candles representing Hasan and Husayn.

1 Oleg Graber, article: "Seeing and Believing," 1, 2. *From the thirteenth century onward, the Muslim world accepted the existence of representations of the Prophet. This iconography was not common, and was usually restricted to the accompaniment of a narrative text, or to serve as pious reminders of an exemplary life. Sometime in the fifteenth century, and certainly by the sixteenth century, it became customary to veil the face of the Prophet.* There seems to have been no judicial ruling approving or opposing visual representation, but Muslims were surrounded in the many areas by religions and culture in which images played a major role. These images are much more often Shia than Sunni. Very few of them come from the Arab world.

2 "...Fatima's Illumination and Divine Grace." See Introduction to poem "One Morning in Sayfad-din's Kitchen," p. 4.

Form: hendecasyllabics

Joy Thief ♦ *p. 38*

This poem is based on these sources: "Ali found her in a dyed gown and said: What's this? She said that the Prophet of God had us do this. He went (to Muhammad) and said: "O, Prophet, I saw Fatima and she was wearing this dyed robe." Muhammad said: "I ordered the people to do that. O, Ali, what makes you cheerful?" Tuysirkani, *Musnad* #134, 245. Also Clohessy, *Fatima*, 45, fn 151.

In this story, Muhammad and Fatima were staying outside Mecca, and Ali arrived from Yemen. He returned and found his wife wearing dyed cloth and was upset. Ibn Kathir, *The Life*, 4: 240.

Form: dactylic tetrameter.

Pregnancy ♦ *p. 40*

1   Clohessy, *Fatima*, 129, 130. Fn 417. [Rawandi, *al Khara'ij*, 2:841. This 12th century source spends two pages describing Fatima's pregnancy in detail.]

2   Ibid., 130. "I felt a crawling on my back, like the crawling of ants…" http://www.news-medical.net/health/Symptoms-of-intrahepatic-cholestasis-of-pregnancy-(ICP).aspx

3   Finch, *An Exhaltation of Forms*, "Sapphics," Grace Schulman p. 132. The trochee has two syllables, the first is accented as in WA-ter, LAN-tern. Sapphics and hendecasyllabics are mostly in trochees.

4   Finch, *A Poet's Ear*, 129.

Form: sapphics.

Fatima Tells of Interruption ♦ *p. 42*

1   Bukhari, *Sahih*, 2, book 21, #227.

Also in Clohessy, *Fatima*, 45, 46.

Also in Suyuti, *Musnad Fatimah*, #52.

Form: ghazal.

While She Sleeps ♦ *p. 44*

1   *Encyclopedia of Fatima*, 17:119, 120. See also Muslim, *The English Translations*, 4, #1701.

Form: iambic pentameter - blank verse.

The Best of Us ♦ *p. 46*

1   Tuysirukani, *Musnad Fatima*, part 1, #137.

Request: a pantoum ✦ *p. 48*

1 Bukhari, *Sahih*, 3, book 47, #755. See also Ibn Sa'd, *The Women,* 8:123-126. G.H.A. Juynboll, p. 197, "Don't you love who I love?" *Encyclopedia of Canonical Hadith.*

Form: The pantoum is an interlocking form composed of groups of four lines. All lines are refrains and often rhyme.

Muhammad's Wounds ✦ *p. 50*

1 Quote on "Islam" spoken by Imam Bilal Hyde.
2 There are at least two Qur'anic verses giving permission to fight.
Permission to fight is given to those against whom war is being wrongfully waged... (and) those who have been driven from their homelands against all right for no other reason than their saying," "our Sustainer is God." [Q. 22:39]. *And fight in God's cause against those who wage war against you, but do not commit aggression...* [Q. 2:190]. Both references: Muhammad Assad, trans., *Qur'an.*
Fatima's role in the Battle of Uhud: Bukhari, *Sahih*, 1, book 4, #244. And 5, book 59, #402.
Ibn Ishaq, *The Life*, 380, 381.
Clohessy, *Fatima,* 25, fn 85.
Form: couplets in iambic hexameter/pentameter, 6/5.

Hamza: *'Amm al-Kabir* ✦ *p. 52*

Hamza, Muhammad's uncle was in the household, and later fought alongside him from the first years of hostility. When Khadija offered herself in marriage to Muhammad... "It was Hamza, whom the Hashimites delegated to represent them on this occasion." Lings, *Muhammad*, 35. When Hamza joined the followers of Islam, Muhammad's enemies were disappointed and concerned. He was a strong leader and fighter. He helped keep Muhammad's family safe over the coming years. He was killed and maimed in the Battle of Uhud. For everyone, especially Fatima this was a terrible loss. She was said to go to his grave often. Ibn Sa'd, *Tabaqat*, 8:11.

1 The story of the *tasbih* of clay beads is mentioned in Ansari, *Encyclopedia of Fatima,* 22:202. Clohessy, *Fatima*, 25, fn 82 quotes historian Qazwini: "Fatima went every Saturday morning to the graves of the martyrs and at Hamza's grave would plead God's mercy and forgiveness for him."

She Cleans the Swords ◆ *p. 54*

1   Belgin Batun, ed., *Osmanli Devletinde,* p. 90.
2   Ibn Kathir, *The Life of the Prophet Muhammad,* 3: 65. Also Ibn Ishaq, *The Life,* 389.

Sword reference with visuals: http://privat.bahnhof.se/wb042294/Bilder/pic_Prophet-swords.html (URL Accessed May, 2016.)
Form: hendecasyllabics.

The Hungry Years ◆ *p. 58*

1   Ibn Sa'd, *The Women,* 15.
2   Ansari, *Encyclopedia of Fatima,* 17:121, 122.
3   Schimmel, *And Muhammad,* 44. *Kusa* – squash that was a favorite food of the Prophet.

Form: iambic tetrameter quatrains.

Camera Obscura ◆ *p. 60*

1   Suyuti, *Musnad Fatima,* #187. Also Ibid., #95, #196, #197, #198.
Bukhari, 4, book 53, #342. Also vol. 7, book 62, #157.
Form: prose poem.

Within the Cloak ◆ *p. 62*

1   Suyuti, *Musnad Fatimah,* #163, 164.
2   Ansari, *Encyclopedia of Fatima,* 19, 373. (more discussion p. 371-386.)
3   Although his granddaughters are not mentioned here, it is possible Fatima was pregnant with her fourth child, Umm Kulthum, aka: *Zaynab as-Sughra* (The Younger Zaynab). "She was born when her grandfather was alive." (No exact dates are given.) Ansari, *Encyclopedia of Fatima al-Zahra* vol. 5, p. 389.
4   Annemarie Schimmel in her book: *And Muhammad is His Messenger,* 19 mentions "the *ahl al-kisa,* the People of the Cloak... Muslim tradition affirms that Muhammad once took them under his robe in order to show that he cared for them in a very special way."

Perfect ◆ *p. 64*

1   Spellberg, D.A., *Politics, Gender,* 174-178.
2   Suyuti, *Musnad Fatimah,* #67.
    Ibid., #63.
Form: dactylic tetrameter.

Safiyya's Friendship ◆ *p. 66*
[1] Kahn, *Untold*, "The Jewish Wives," 84, 85.
[2] Ibn Saʾd, *The Women of Medina*, 90. "Safiyya bint Huyayy came with some gold earrings and gave them to Fatima...." For additional connection between Fatima and Safiyya see the following reference: Dakake, *The Charismatic Community*, 217. "The Prophet said that in the event of his death, Safiyya should be taken in and cared for by Ali (and Fatima)."

Her House ◆ *p. 68*
[1] Ibn Kathir, *The Life of the Prophet Muhammad*, 2:208
[2] Halman, *Where the Two Seas Meet*, xvii and 55. This gives information on Khidr.
[3] Ansari, *Encyclopedia of Fatima*, 4: 12, 11, 14, 30.

Demolished ◆ *p. 70*
Islamica Magazine, issue 15, 2006. "The House of Sayyida Khadija," with photographs. When *Islamica* became an on-line magazine and posted past issues—this article was missing. Fortunately I have an original non-digital issue with the story and pictures.

[1] Lecture: "The House of Khadija," University of London May 11, 2000, Ahmed Zaki Yameni, Director of the excavation, photography and re-burial in 1989. URL accessed at April, 2012, then May, 2016: (see comments below). <http://www.youtube.com/watch?v=Fcx-fJCCy3I>

In 2012 when I watched this lecture and took careful notes, the speaker explained the reason for covering with sand and cement after excavation as follows: "The house may encourage idolatry," and The house can be regarded as "a blessing object attracting who knows what people." This very same URL from 2000 I used in 2012, filmed on the same date, takes you to a lecture which has *quietly changed*. The podium has the initials SOAS (School of Oriental and African Studies), yet is no mention of The University of London, where the first lecture took place, only Al-Furqan Islamic Heritage Foundation. The above quotes used in my poem are no longer spoken by Director Yameni. In the first lecture he mentions how his wife was brought to see the work, but viewed the site from inside a building above, while he went into the excavated rooms below with his son, before the "clean sand" and cement closure covered the house of

Khadija. I heard no word of any of this in the talk with the same URL. This is not a surprise, since the on-line *Islamica Magazine* seems to have lost the article on the famous house.

Scent ◆ *p. 74*

[1] Ansari, *Encyclopedia of Fatima*, 20:527.

[2] Schimmel, *And Muhammad*, 51, 52. "God has made dear to me from your world women and fragrance, and the joy of my eyes is in prayer." This is a famous *hadith* by Prophet Muhammad.

myrtle—Skinner, *Myths and legends*, 51. "To the Persians, Jews and Arabs, *myrtle* was a symbol of paradise. In biblical stories, Adam chose to take the myrtle plant when he was expelled from the Garden of Eden."

Muhammad's Death ◆ *p. 76*

For a description of Muhammad's death see Lings, *Muhammad*, 341.

Blue Date Cake: Fatima's Story ◆ *p. 78*

Tuysirukani, *Al-Musnad*, #252.

Ansari, *Encyclopedia of Fatima*, 9:254, 255.

Form: rhyming iambic stanzas. After the poem by Marilyn Hacker: "Letter on August 15" *from Love, Death and the Changing of the Seasons*, 185. (Metrical iambic arrangement after James Wright).

The Sermon ◆ *p. 80*

[1] See George William Warner, "Tragedy, History, and the Sacred: The *Hujjah* of Fatima al-Zahra," in *Journal of Shi'a Islamic Studies*, 4/2/11, 153. This paper talks of Fatima's role as "the echo of her father, the one who receives the whole prophetic message as his inheritor..." 155. (this is an internal position that would never be recognized in the paternalistic culture.)

[2] Ibid., 158.

One Reason ◆ *p. 82*

In Fatima's speech at the mosque: "She argued strongly for her right to inheritance, using Qur'anic verses to prove her claims to it..." Osman, *Female Personalities*, 184, fn 128.

For this *hadith* see Madelung, *The Succession*, 50, 51 as well as Juynboll, *Encyclopedia of the Canonical Hadith*, 707. Caliph Abu Bakr said: "I

heard the Messenger of God say, "We do not leave a heritage, whatever we leave must be alms." Also Bukhari, *Sahih,* 4, book 53, #325.
Form: rhyming iambic quatrains address this formal moment; after A.E. Stallings: "Empty Icon Frame."

Ali Says Goodbye ◆ *p. 84*
Tabari, *The History,* 39:167.

Letters of Love ◆ *p. 86*
[1]   This account is found in: Ansari, *Encyclopedia of Fatima,* 9:252, 253. Also see Khan, The Sufi Message, 11:166: "…the *Rasul* is the one who represents God's perfection through human limitation."
Houri – an angelic being
Muhammadan rasul Allah: Muhammad is the Messenger of God.
Form: hendecasyllabics.

Glory ◆ *p. 88*
[1]   Clohessy, *Fatima,* 168. Also description of Fatima and paradise in Suyuti, *Musnad Fatima,* #73, #91, #92.
[2]   Form: dactylic tetrameter is mentioned here in Finch, *An Exaltation,* "Dactylic Meter," 67.
Also "the many sounding sea,"(*polyphosbiou thalassa*) Greek, from Homer, 66.

Replaced ◆ *p. 90*
[1]   For Muhammad's quote about Hasan see: Majlisi, *Bihar al-Anwar,* 43:294.
Reflections of Hasan's childhood: "I saw the Prophet while al-Hasan was on his shoulders and the Prophet was saying, 'O Allah I love him! May You love him too.'" In Bukhari, *Sahih,* 9:432.
In his the inaugural talk, Hasan spoke with a speech defect, but with eloquence. The people were moved.
[2]   He quoted Qu'ran [Q.43:23]. Found in Madelung, *The Succession,* 311, 312.
After Hasan the leadership passed to Muawiyah, then his son Yazid, who had Husayn killed.

Moon ◆ *p. 92*

[1] Nasr, *The Shia Revival*, 33.

Ibid, 34. Some of the cities where mourning marches for Husayn take place: Lahore, Lucknow, Tehran, Karbala, Bahrain, Nabatiye.

[2] Hyder, *Reliving Karbala*, p. 14. Quote in Urdu from Sikh poet, Kanwar Mahender Singh Bedi.

Muharram: First month of the Islamic calendar, the *Mourning of Muharram* is associated with the Martyrdom of Husayn at Karbala on Ashura, the 10th day of Muharram, 680 CE.

Winter Landscape ◆ *p. 94*

Last Light Breaking, the Death of Husayn ◆ *p. 96*

[1] Title from lines of the poem by Dylan Thomas: "A Refusal to Mourn the Death, by Fire of a Child in London."

[2] Safi, *Memories of Muhammad*, 220.

[3] Hyder, *Reliving Karbala*, 134.

Form: iambic pentameter and hexameter in couplets.

Shahrbanu and the Royal Fabric ◆ *p. 98*

[1] For information on Shahrbanu and her relationship to Persian and Arab history see David Pinault, "Zaynab bint Ali and the place of the Women of the Households of the First Imams in Shi'ite Devotional Literature." 80-82. Also: Amir-Moezzi, *The Spirituality of Shi'i Islam*, 45-49.

Form: hendecasyllabics.

Standing Tall ◆ *p. 100*

Introductory epigraph: Marilyn Hacker, "Ghazal: A Woman."

A good source on Fatima's daughters is David Pinault: "Zaynab bint Ali and the place of the Women of the Households of the First Imams in Shi'ite Devotional Literature," 82, 83.

The daughters, Zaynab and Umm Kulthum, were said to survive Karbala, the location of the terrible massacre of their brother Husayn and his family and followers, 680 CE. Some write of the sisters brought as prisoners to the Caliph in Damascus. Zaynab is famous for speaking harshly to Yazid, condemning him and his rule as Umayyid Caliph— the man who ordered the slaughter and took over Husayn's rule.

Umm Kulthum, the younger sister, is most commonly mentioned in terms of whom she married, or did not marry, and very rarely for her accomplishments. Madelung, *The Succession,* 67, 79.

Form: tercets (three stanzas), iambic pentameter.

Lioness ◆ *p. 102*

[1] George William Warner, "Tragedy, History, and the Sacred: The *Hujjah* of Fatima al-Zahra," *Journal of Shi'a Islamic Studies,* 4/2/11, 158.

[2] Ibn Ishaq, *The Life of Muhammad,* 59. This refers to Salama, wife of the Prophet's great-grandfather Hashim from Mecca. She was a woman from Medina. He returned home and she remained behind to give birth and raise their child 'Abd al-Muttalib. When Hashim died, his brother went to bring the adolescent to live with his father's family in Mecca. Salama and Hashim's brother negotiated for three days. The boy said he would only leave his mother if she told him to, which she finally did. So he was taken to live in Mecca. When he was an old man, he raised his grandson, Muhammad.

Muhammad's mother, Amina stayed with her birth family during her marriage and pregnancy. She died when the boy was seven or eight. He then became an orphan and lived with relatives as he grew up.

The information on *al-Uzza* comes from Ibn Sa'd, *The Women of Medina,* vol. VIII, p. 9.

Over Damascus ◆ *p. 104*

On the building the words: *Salam Great Zaynab* are in elegant Arabic, each letter shines with lights.

Hyder, *Reliving Karbala,* 96, 97: information on Zaynab's sermon.

A version of the Speech in the court of Yazid is found here: (URL accessed May, 2016.)

https://www.religiousforums.com/threads/lady-zainab-a-s-speech-in-the-court-of-yazid.85730/

There was a rocket attack on the Shrine of Sayyida Zaynab in the suburbs of Damascus on Friday (July 19, 2013) as part of the Syrian Civil War. Shrapnel killed the venerated caretaker of the shrine and his grandson.

January 31, 2016, two suicide bombs and a car bomb exploded in the town of *Sayyidah Zaynab* near the Sayyidah Zaynab Mosque (six miles south of Damascus). At least 60 people were killed and another

110 people were wounded in the explosions. On February 21, 2016 more explosions and death.

"Nurses Day" is celebrated annually in Iran on February 25 in honor of Sayyida Zaynab's birth.

Form: sonnet.

Almost Nothing, With a Beauty All Its Own ◆ *p. 106*

1 Ibn Sa'd, *The Women*, 8:299. Umm Kulthum may have married Umar ibn al-Khattab when she had reached puberty, and it is written that they had a child named Zayd and one named Ruqayya. Umar bragged about the marriage: "Congratulate me! I wanted to have this as well." Also this: Madelung, *The Succession to Muhammad*, 79: "Umar's demand, during his caliphate, to marry Muhammad's granddaughter, Umm Kulthum, Ali's daughter, was an assertion of his having reached a social status he had not enjoyed during Muhammad's lifetime."

2 Ansari, *Encyclopedia of Fatima*, 5:389. There was a nickname for Umm Kulthum: *Zaynab a-Sughra* (the younger Zaynab). Umm Kulthum died the same year as her sister, Zaynab, in 662CE.

3 This quote is from the article by David Pinault: "Zaynab bint Ali and the place of the Women of the Households of the First Imams in Shi'ite Devotional Literature," 82. Umm Kulthum says: "The children of prophets aren't meant to be slaves of the children of bastards and pretenders." (The words refer to those at the court of Yazid, who ordered the slaughter of her brother Husayn and others at Karbala.)

4 Ansari, *Encyclopedia of Fatima*, 5:389, 394. The Ambassador to Byzantium said: "She is majestic, more so than The Queen of Byzantium." and "Umm Kulthum wrote a great deal of eloquent poetry and she is buried in Medina."

Form: prose poem.

This Tree ◆ *p. 108*

Ali begins the line of teaching authority in all "family trees" in the lineages of Sufism. The woman leaders have been excluded, from lineage lists, and are only named in books. Rabia of Basra is considered to be an important woman saint of Islam, eighth century.

Form: dactylic tetrameter.

In Flight ◆ *p. 110*

A Call and Response ◆ *p. 112*

Quote: "Whoever pleases…," Translated by Camille Adams Helminski in her book, *Women of Sufism*, p. 11. Also: Ansari, *Encyclopedia of Fatima*, 21:327. Prophet Muhammad, refers to Fatima, "She is from my flesh, the light of my eye and the fruit of my heart."
The *Encyclopedia Iranica:*
i. In History and Shi'ite Hagiography and ii. In Myth, Folklore and Popular Devotion. This article compiled by Jean Calmard, 1999 Print version: Vol. IX, Fasc. 4, 400-404.
http://www.iranicaonline.org/articles/fatema. (URL accessed July, 2016.)
Khidr – more information in the introductory paragraph for poem "Her House," p. 68.

Bibliography

SU (Sunni), SH (Shia), and SF (Sufi) initials are placed at the end of the listed book or article, when the sources used here speak from that perspective.

Amir-Moezzi, Mohammad 'Ali, *The Spirituality of Shi'i Islam*. London, I.B.Tauris Publishers, 2011. SH

— "Fatema: In History and Shia Hagiography." *Encyclopedia Iranica*, (On line Shia, Iranian reference accessed at May, 2016: http://www. iranicaonline.org/articles/fatema)

Ansari al-Zanjani al-Khu'ini, Isma'il, *Al-Mawsu'a al-Kubrá 'an Fatima al-Zahra (Encyclopedia of Fatima al-Zahra)*. 25 vols. Qum: Dalil-i Ma, 2008. SH

Aslan, Reza, *No god but God*. NY, Random House, 2006.

Aydin, Himli, in Belgin Batun, ed. *Osmanli Devletinde, Ehl-I Beyt Sevgisi*. (Collection of articles sponsored by the Topkapi Museum and Türkkad). Istanbul, Nefes Yayim Lare, 2008.

Bukhari, Muhammad ibn Ismail Bukhari, *Sahih al-Bukhari*. Translation: Muhammad Muhsin Khan. 9 vols. Alexandria, VA, Al-Sadawi Publications, 1996. SU

Burckhart, John Lewis, *Arabic Proverb*. Mineola, N.Y. 2004, Dover Publications (originally published by J. Murray, London, 1830).

Clohessy, Christopher Paul, *Fatima, Daughter of Muhammad*. Piscataway, N.J. Gorgias Press, 2009. SH, SU

Dakake, Maria Massi, *The Charismatic Community; Shi'ite Identity in Early Islam*. Albany, NY. State University of New York Press, 2008. SH

Desert Tracings: Six Classic Arabian Odes by Alqama, Shanfara, Labid, Antara, Asha, and Dhu Rumma. Translated and Introduced by Michael Sells. Middletown, Connecticut, Wesleyan University Press, 1989.

Early Arabic Poetry: Select Poems. Edited, translated, with commentary by Alan Jones, UK, Ithaca Press, 2011.

Encyclopedia of Muhammad's Women Companions and the Traditions they Related. Shaykh Muhammad Hisham Kabbani + Laleh Bakhtiar. Chicago, Kazi Publications, 1998. SU

Finch, Annie, *A Poet's Ear: A Handbook of Meter and Form,* Ann Arbor, MI, The University of Michigan Press, 2013.

— *An Exaltation of Forms, Contemporary Poets Celebrate the Diversity of Their Art.* Edited by Annie Finch and Katherine Varnes. Ann Arbor, MI, The University of Michigan Press, 2002.

Graber, Oleg, article: "Seeing and Believing." New Republic Magazine, October, 2009.

Halman, Hugh Talat, *Where the Two Seas Meet: The Qur'anic Story of al-Kidr and Moses in Sufi Commentaries as a Model of Spiritual Guidance.* Louisville, KY, Fons Vitae Press, 2013. SF

Helminski, Camille Adams, *Women of Sufism.* Boston, Shambhala, 2003. SF

Hyder, Syed Akbar, Reliving Karbala: Martyrdom in South Asian Memory, UK, Oxford University Press, 2006. SH

Ibn Ishaq, *The Life of Muhammad.* Translated by A. Guillaume. New York, Oxford University Press, 2003. SU

Ibn Kathir, *The Life of the Prophet Muhammad, Sira al-Nabawiyya.* Translated by Trevor Le Gassick. 4 Vols. Reading, UK, Garnet Publications, 2000. SU

Ibn Sa'd, Muhammad, *Kitab al-Tabaqat al-Kabir* in 11 volumes. Vol. 8, *The Women of Medina* was translated by Aisha Bewley, London, Ta-Ha Publications, 1997. SU

Juynboll, G.H.A. *Encyclopedia of the Canonical Hadith.* Leiden, The Netherlands, Koninklij Brill NV. 2007.

Kahn, Tamam, *Untold, A History of the Wives of Prophet Muhammad.* NY, Monkfish Books, 2010. SF

Khan, Hazrat Inayat, *The Sufi Message.* 12 vols. Delhi, Morilal Banarsidass Publications, 1990. SF

Lane, E.W., *Arabic ~ English Lexicon.* 2 vols. Cambridge, England, The Islamic Texts Society, 1984.

Lings, Martin, *Muhammad.* NY, Inner Traditions International, Ltd. 1983. SU, SF

Madelung, Wilferd, *The Succession to Muhammad.* UK, Cambridge University Press, 1997. SU and SH

Majlisi, Muhammad Baqir., *Zindigani-yi Hadrat-i Zahra: tarjama-yi jild-i 43 Bihar al-anwar.* Translation by Muhammad Qa'im Fard. Qumm, Dalil-i Ma, 2012. SH

Muslim, Sahih, *The English Translations of Sahih Muslim*. Translation by Nasiruddin al-Khattab. 7 vols. Saudi Arabia, Dar-us-Salam Publications, 2007. SU

Nasr, Valli, *The Shia Revival, How Conflicts with Islam Will Shape the Future*. NY, Norton, 2007. SH

Night & Horses & the Desert, An Anthology of Classical Arabic Literature, edited by Robert Irwin. NY, Anchor Books, Random House, 2001.

Osman, Rawand, *Female Personalities in the Qur'an and Sunna: Examining the Major Sources of Imami Shi'i Islam*. Hoboken, NJ, Taylor and Francis Publications, 2014. SH

Pinault, David, "Zaynab bint Ali and the place of the Women of the Households of the First Imams in Shi'ite Devotional Literature." *Women in the Medieval Islamic World*, edited by Gavin R.G. Hambly. London, Macmillan Press, 1999. SH

Pinckney-Stretkevych, Suzanne, *The Mute Immortals Speak*. Ithaca, NY, Cornell University Press, 1993.

Qur'an: The Message of the Qur'an. Translated by Muhammad Asad. Bristol, UK, The Book Foundation, 2003.

Safi, Omid, *Memories of Muhammad*, SF. Harper One, 2009.

Schimmel, Annemarie, *And Muhammad Is His Messenger*. Chapel Hill, NC. UNC Press, 1985.

Skinner, Charles M. *Myths and legends of Flowers, Trees, Fruits and Plants*. The Netherlands, Fredonia Books, 2002.

Spellberg, Denise, *Politics, Gender, and the Islamic Past*. NY, Columbia University Press, 1994.

Suyuti, Jalaluddin. *Musnad Fatimah al-Zahra wa-ma warad fi fadliha,* edited by Fawaz Ahmad Zamarli. Beirut, Dar Ibn Hazm, 1994. SU

Tabari, Abu Ja'far Muhammad, *The History of al-Tabari* in 39 volumes. Vol. 9 "The Last Years of the Prophet," Translated by Ishmael K. Poonqwala, NY. State University of New York Press, 1990. SU

— *The History of al-Tabari*, vol. 39, "Biographies of the Prophet's Companions and Their Successors," Translated by Ella Landau-Tasseron, NY. State University of New York Press, 1998. SU

— *Jāmi' al-Bayan an ta wil ay al-Qur'an*. vol. 22. *Jāmi' al-Bayan is in 16* vols. edited by Mahmūd Muhammad Shākir. Dar al-ma'arif, Cairo, 1969. SU

Tuysirkani, Husayn al-Islami, *Musnad Fatimat Zahra*. Beirut: Dar al-Safwa, 1992. SH

Warner, George William, "Tragedy, History, and the Sacred: The *Hujjah* of Fatima al-Zahra." *Journal of Shi'a Islamic Studies*, 4:2, 2011. SH

Thanks to the editors of the following journals and anthologies in which these poems or earlier versions first appeared:

Knot Magazine: Spring 2016, The Fatima Sequence: "Scent," "While She Sleeps," "Gift of Prayer," "Request: a pantoum," "Within the Cloak."

The Wide Shore: Issue 2 (Fall, 2015), "Fatima… Ever After: From the Encyclopedia Iranica."(changed to "The Call and Response.")

Snapdragon: A Journal of Art and Healing, March, 2016, "Blue Date Cake."

Aji Magazine, Fall, 2015, "In Flight." Spring, 2016: "Sacred Names," "Jinn," and "Camera Obscura."

HCE, of Silhouette Press, UK, April, 2016, *Blood and Water* Issue. "She Cleans the Swords."

Mezzo Cammin: Online Journal of Formalist Poetry by Women, Vol. 9, Issue 2: "Fruit of the Heart," "This Tree," "Joy Thief."

Adanna Literary Journal: Women and Food Issue: "Planned Famine: Mecca Around the Year 615."

Soul-Making-Keats Literary Competition, Sonnet Award, 2013, "Fatima Tells of Muhammad's Death" (changed to "Muhammad's Death.")

Complete Word: Fatima al-Zahra Poems: "Glory," "Silver Hand," "Wild Honey of Adab," "Shine."

https://completeword.wordpress.com//?s=Fatima+Poems+updated&search=Go (URL accessed July, 2016)